From Charity
to Equity

From Charity to Equity

Race, Homelessness,
and Urban Schools

Ann M. Aviles de Bradley

Foreword by Marvin Lynn

TEACHERS COLLEGE PRESS

TEACHERS COLLEGE | COLUMBIA UNIVERSITY

NEW YORK AND LONDON

Published by Teachers College Press, 1234 Amsterdam Avenue, New York, NY 10027

Library of Congress Cataloging-in-Publication Data is available at loc.gov

Aviles de Bradley, Ann M.
    From charity to equity : race, homelessness, and urban schools / Ann M. Aviles de Bradley.
        pages cm
    Includes bibliographical references and index.
    ISBN 978-0-8077-5639-3 (pbk. : alk. paper) —
    ISBN 978-0-8077-7371-0 (e-book)
        1. Homeless children—Education—United States. 2. Homeless youth—Education—United States. 3. Educational sociology. 4. Discrimination in education—United States. 5. Educational equalization—United States. 6. Urban education—United States. I. Title.
    LC5144.2.B73 2015
    379.2'60973—dc23   2015003168

ISBN 978-0-8077-5639-3 (paper)
ISBN 978-0-8077-7371-0 (ebook)

Printed on acid-free paper
Manufactured in the United States of America

22   21   20   19   18   17   16   15   8   7   6   5   4   3   2   1

Contents

Foreword

After I read Ann Aviles de Bradley's *From Charity to Equity*, I was more enlightened than I have been in a long time regarding the plight of poor African American and Latina/o students in beleaguered urban public school systems like the Chicago Public Schools. I was also completely devastated. Like Leon, one of the main subjects in her book, I attended Chicago Public Schools and benefited from the free lunch program. According to the USDA's standards, both Leon and I lived below the poverty line. However, there was one key difference between myself and the students featured in Aviles de Bradley's incredible book: I *always* had stable housing. Not only am I an African American male who experienced poverty in the very school system about which Aviles de Bradley writes, I have also contributed greatly to the research on race and education through the publication of several articles and a well-received edited book on the topic (see Lynn & Dixson, 2013). Even with all my experiential and academic knowledge, I was devastated to learn of the experiences of these young people in what many call the richest nation in the world. As close as I'm sure I came during the 12 years or so I attended Chicago Public Schools to experiencing what these students experienced, what I learned from reading this book was completely outside of the realm of my experience. I was even more devastated to learn that their teachers and administrators were either blind to their problems or powerless to do much to help them.

I am forever changed by my experience with *From Charity to Equity*. The book clearly and beautifully chronicles the experiences of unaccompanied homeless youth of color and incorporates important perspectives of their teachers and administrators while providing a keen critical race analysis of the social and political context of education in what Pauline Lipman disparaging refers to as "the global city." It is meticulously researched and well framed. Aviles de Bradley's work is a great triumph. It is a great testament to the power of qualitative research. The stories of these students, their families, and their teachers are riveting and groundbreaking.

The work is reminiscent of great work by sociologist Elliott Liebow, who first published with *Tally's Corner* in 1967. His work humanized Black street corner men by bringing their stories to light in a way that had never been done before. Through Liebow's work, we came to understand these men's perspectives on inequality and everyday life. The same is true for Aviles de Bradley's bold interdisciplinary work. We understand the lives of homeless students and their teachers in ways that we had not previously understood them. This work can and should change the educational research community. It should be required reading for all teacher education, social work, educational leadership and counseling programs. I feel honored to have been asked to write this foreword.

—Marvin Lynn

Preface

Housing instability and homelessness among children and youth continues to rise. Despite significant increases, the issue of homelessness among students receives little attention. Further, the majority of practicing teachers and teacher educators are unaware of McKinney–Vento and its mandates. This situation leaves many students experiencing homelessness with little to no support or access to their educational rights. The aim of this book is to create awareness among schools, teachers, teacher educators, and the general public. With this awareness, my hope is that more individuals are compelled to act. The students' stories and experiences described here will likely upset, sadden, and awe the reader simultaneously. The stories of the youth may evoke feelings of sympathy; I respectfully ask that you resist these feelings. The youth experiencing homelessness that I have worked with over the years are not looking for sympathy; they seek stability, respect, educational access, and an educational system that honors and supports their efforts to remain engaged in school and reach their fullest potential. This book seeks to contribute to the ongoing conversation regarding opportunities and support for individuals experiencing homelessness and their pursuit for educational equity and justice. Inequitable systems and structures (particularly those related to class and race) pervasive in U.S. society must be critically examined and fundamentally changed; this is the work to be engaged if there is to be a significant decrease in the number of students forced into homeless situations as well as equal treatment and access for those individuals.

This book begins with an overview of the topics and issues that influence and shape access, opportunities, and educational options for youth experiencing homelessness/instability. Chapter 2 then centers the perspectives and voices of the youth, increasing readers' understanding of the educational and life experiences of students identified as homeless. Their voices speak to the topics outlined in Chapter 1. Further, their voices provide a human face to issues and topics that are too often discussed in a theoretical and/or objective manner. Chapter 3 provides a space for the adults to share their insights and understanding of the experience of the youth, and their comprehension and assessment of McKinney–Vento policy in school, educational, and social contexts. Illuminating the issues and connecting them to the youth and adults most impacted by McKinney–Vento allow for the generation of analysis of those topics and suggestions for increasing our awareness of the pervasiveness of homelessness among youth, what educators and others can do to address this critical phenomenon, and factors to contend with for improved practices at the school, district, and national levels (Chapter 4). Finally, the epilogue addresses a postproject encounter with one of the students and the manner in which this work seeks to promote increased awareness, accountability, and justice with and for students experiencing homelessness.

A qualitative research approach offered the tools needed to examine homeless education policy in the school context, providing further insight into policy adherence, implementation, and accountability or the lack thereof at the school level. While the stories of the students are at the center of my inquiry, context assists in understanding the ways in which the larger world has impacted students' experiences with homelessness and education. This book includes a specific focus on the manner in which race and racism are discussed and/or omitted from homeless education policy and discourse. All school and participant names are pseudonyms to preserve the anonymity of the schools and participants.

Acknowledgments

I owe a debt of gratitude to the many individuals who have been integral to the creation of this book. First and foremost, this work would not have been possible without the students. I am so thankful you allowed me into your lives—your strength, humility, and resilience are what motivate me to continue this work. Thank you to all the students, teachers, administrators, staff, and advocates for your openness, encouragement, and belief in this work and the possibilities of its reach.

As this book is the result of my doctoral dissertation, I am forever grateful to my advisor, dissertation chair, and friend, David O. Stovall—your faith and support in this work has been invaluable to its completion. I also owe much gratitude to my entire committee: Dr. Laurie Schaffner, Dr. David Mayrowetz, Dr. Patricia Popp, and Dr. Pamela Quiroz. Thank you for your sincere and candid feedback on the writing/research process. I am also thankful for the many colleagues, friends, and family members that have read drafts of this work and provided me with great insight and assistance, both formally and informally: William Ayers, Richard Benson, Gabriel Cortez, Kay Fujiyoshi, Ronald Hallett, Christine Helfrich, Jessica Heybach, Laurene Heybach, Dan Hibbler, Anne Holcomb, Nicole Holland, JoEllen (Ellie) Hutchinson, Angelique Kelly-Lara, Leo Lara, Crystal Laura, Marvin Lynn, Eleni Makris, Ebony McGhee, Erica Meiners, Peter Miller, Richard Milner, Dominique Montague, Patricia Nix-Hodes, Isaura Pulido, Patricia Rivera, Tanya Royster, Brian Schultz, Jennifer Tsamoulos, Durene Wheeler, Karlisa Williams, and Kirstin Williams. A special thank you to my cousin, colleague, and friend, Erica Davila, who has provided support and love for my work, sanity, and overall development. To my partner and friend, Keith Bradley, who has provided unwavering support, critical feedback, and love: Thank you for your understanding, patience, and thoughtfulness on many late nights, early mornings, and weekends. I will forever be grateful for the foundation of love and care provided to me by my parents, siblings, grandparents, children, nieces, nephews, aunts, uncles, and cousins (who are too many to name, but you all know who you are)—without you all I know this work would not be possible. There are so many others that I have crossed paths with; be it in shared community or more formal spaces, these encounters have contributed to my work and development, and I want to thank the village that is my community for giving me the strength and encouragement to see this project through.

To the many organizations and to folks within them, the experiences provided in each of these spaces have been integral to my growth both professionally and personally: University of Illinois at Chicago, Northeastern Illinois University, Latin American Recruitment Educational Services, Institute for Research on Race and Public Policy-Dissertation Associates, Chicago State University, Alliance of Black and Latina/o Graduate Students, Diversifying Faculty in Illinois, Puerto Rican Studies Association, Write-on-Site groups, 2nd Legislative Educational Advisory Committee, The Night Ministry, Open Door Shelter, Family Rescue, Chicago Coalition for the Homeless, St. Leonard's Adult High School, Critical Race Studies in Education Association, Wu-Writing Crew, Chicago Grassroots Curriculum TaskForce, The Illinois McKinney-Vento Network, and La Phoenikera Writers' Guild (LaPWG). I am thankful for your collective knowledge and insight; it has made all the difference.

I am also thankful to everyone at Teachers College Press for all of their work, dedication, and support in making this book a reality.

CHAPTER 1

Introduction

I was first introduced to the reality of homelessness among youth while completing fieldwork as an occupational therapy student at a transitional housing agency for women and children who had become homeless due to domestic violence. While working with the women and their children, it became apparent that the majority of the children receiving services were aged 12 and younger. When I naively asked, "Where are the older kids?" staff replied, "At shelters for youth" (I had never heard of youth shelters nor knew of any). This interaction prompted my journey into the investigation of homelessness among youth.

Shortly thereafter, I contacted New Opportunities Shelter (NOS), an agency that serves unaccompanied homeless youth aged 14 to 21 in the city of Chicago. I began collaborating with a social worker, conducting a life-skills group for the youth residing at NOS. In group meetings, these young people discussed many issues related to adolescent development and how to manage "adult" responsibilities such as getting a job, renting an apartment, obtaining medical care for themselves, and, for some, their children too. The youth knew a whole lot about what they needed to become more adept at caring for themselves; however, they were not provided consistent guidance and support to obtain these skills due to severed and/or tumultuous relationships with their parents/guardians.

Many of the young people shared their stories, such as the joys of having a first child; the reality of having to be the sole provider for their child or children; and the abuse, neglect, and conflict that led to their becoming homeless. Despite their past and current situations, they all wanted what most people want—to be "successful" in life. When asked where they would like to be 5, 10 years from now, many responded that they would like to "finish school," "get a job," "buy a house." When prompted to share more about their plans to meet these goals, almost always I would hear "go back to school," "get my GED," "go to college." Although they would readily admit that they didn't like school or didn't see it as a priority due to other, more pressing issues they had in their lives, they viewed

1

education as their ticket out of homelessness. It seemed so simple. But for youth who become homeless, going back to school or maintaining school attendance is complicated. Alberto, a youth residing at NOS, expressed the challenges he was facing with school attendance and engagement:

> I wake up at 5:20 a.m., shower, eat breakfast, and leave to school, it's a 1-1/2 to 2 hour commute each way, I have to take a bus and a train to get to school. Right now with my current situation [being homeless] it's a little awkward, like I have to push myself a lot to be able to do it because, I'm falling asleep in school and it's a bit of a distance to travel every morning . . . I'm having such a difficult time being in school in general, and it does take a lot, my situation, and I don't know, honestly I don't know how I'm doing. . . . It's difficult to concentrate . . . with the issues of being homeless, and being a far distance from my original school makes it a problem that I can't concentrate in school. (Aviles, 2001)

Hearing this account from Alberto and similar accounts from others in the group, I wondered if schools were aware of their situations, and, if so, what were they doing to help? The shelter provided stability, housing, and assistance to get to and from school; however, shelter staff didn't have the resources (human or monetary) to address the issues Alberto and other youth experiencing instability were facing, such as not being able to concentrate in school because of their unstable living situation.

Legislation addresses educational rights and services for homeless children and youth. This is known as the McKinney–Vento Act, referred to in this book as McKinney–Vento policy or simply McKinney–Vento, and this book explores how that legislatively mandated policy is understood and implemented—or not—by school officials and staff. When asked, teachers and principals are often unaware of or have never heard of McKinney–Vento, but those interviewed shared how they had addressed the challenges encountered by homeless students seeking to maintain school attendance and attainment. These approaches ranged from teachers raising money to help students with school fees, clothing, and so forth, to advocating on students' behalf due to a school attempting to deny them enrollment. These were issues addressed by the McKinney–Vento policy, which states that schools are required to ensure access for students experiencing homelessness. So why were teachers and principals not aware of this policy? Why was it not being implemented? Learning about the experiences of students as well as the lack of awareness about McKinney–Vento amongst teachers and principals led me to a research project that would aid in understanding these current conditions, which persist in spite of the fact that a policy had been created to facilitate educational attainment for homeless children and youth.

More specifically, I was interested in learning about the perspectives and experiences of unaccompanied youth experiencing housing instability. Students defined as "homeless" also include students living in doubled-up situations where their families have moved in with others, as well as students staying in shelters, but the particular group identified as "unaccompanied homeless students" often live on their own, experience significant instability, and receive minimal (if any) support from a consistent, caring adult, often due to tumultuous familial relationships or because family members themselves are experiencing housing instability. In an effort to understand the perspectives of the students experiencing homelessness, I spent one full academic year in two Chicago public schools: Diversey High and Grand High. Spending time in these schools provided the opportunity to interact with unaccompanied homeless students as well as the school- and community-based adults charged with supporting their needs as outlined under McKinney–Vento. Moreover, the interactions, observations, and interviews contribute to a more complex understanding of what it means to be homeless; the need for stronger policy language, implementation, and accountability; the various institutional and social factors that shape the experiences of unaccompanied homeless youth; and the ways in which schools and society can better support students' academic engagement and resiliency as they navigate their academic and social worlds.

STUDENTS EXPERIENCING HOMELESSNESS

Nationally, between 1.6 and 2.8 million youth are homeless in a given year (Hammer, Finkelhor, & Sedlak, 2002; Murphy & Tobin, 2011). Five to 7% of American youth become homeless in any given year (National Alliance to End Homelessness, 2006). The Illinois State Board of Education reported a record 54,892 students experiencing homelessness in the state of Illinois for the 2012–2013 school year (Chicago Coalition for the Homeless [CCH], 2014). Chicago Public Schools identified 18,669 homeless students in the 2012–2013 school year, an 8.2% increase from the prior year. Of these students, 98.3% were children of color and 2,512 were unaccompanied homeless youth (CCH, 2013a). As the number of students experiencing homelessness in Chicago and in other large and small cities across the country continues to rise, it is imperative that districts, schools, teachers, and other stakeholders understand and address the myriad of issues that prevent and/or limit the educational engagement of homeless students. Furthermore, due to the overwhelming predominance of students of color experiencing homelessness, this book examines the role race plays in schools' understanding and willingness or indifference to implementing policy for unaccompanied students of color experiencing homelessness in schools.

Illinois, and more specifically Chicago, has a contentious relationship with McKinney–Vento. In 1992 a massive complaint on behalf of homeless children and families was filed in Chicago against the Illinois State Board of Education (ISBE) and Chicago Public Schools (CPS), known as *Salazar v. Edwards*. (Salazar is the surname of one of the 18 families that brought suit against CPS and ISBE; John Edwards was the state coordinator for the homeless education program at ISBE at the time the lawsuit was filed.) The problems homeless students and their families faced was the alleged failure of CPS to do the following:

1. Allow homeless children to remain in their neighborhood schools when they lost their housing
2. Allow homeless children to enroll without production of records or proof of immunization
3. Allow homeless children to attend the schools and activities that other children attend, including preschool and kindergarten
4. Provide transportation assistance to students
5. Forbid discrimination in services to homeless children
6. Notify homeless families of their education rights and provide a system for homeless parents to appeal any decisions the schools make which may be unfair to homeless children (*Salazar v. Edwards*, 1996)

Although CPS made improvements in identifying and serving homeless students, settling the lawsuit in 1999 (*Salazar v. Edwards*, 1999), substantive problems persisted, as the policy was not properly enforced in many schools, and hence the case returned to the courts for proper enforcement and monitoring (*Salazar v. Edwards*, 2000, 2004). Further, Illinois initiated its own legislation, the Illinois Education for Homeless Children Act (ILEHC), also known as "Charlie's Law," to address the education of homeless children. This law took effect in 1995. Much of the act is similar to the McKinney Act of 1987 but is clearer in certain ways, such as with regard to a parent's choice of schools, transportation assistance, enrollment, and dispute resolution, including the appeal process and a parent's right to sue a school (ILEHC, 1994). The Illinois Education for Homeless Children Act does not free schools from the obligations of the McKinney Act (later the McKinney–Vento Act of 2001); it was meant to provide a more specific written policy to address ambiguities within the act (ILEHC, 1994).

Given the corporatization of public education and the subsequent school closings in Chicago and other cities, youth of color find themselves at a further disadvantage (Farmer et al., 2013). The recent Chicago school closings and the lack of funding, services, and support all contribute to and perpetuate the marginalization of students experiencing homelessness (Chicago Educational Facilities Task Force [CEFTF], 2014). Minority and low-income children were disproportionately impacted by school closings/actions in Chicago: Eighty-eight percent of students impacted by school closings were African American, and 93% were low income, as compared to 42% African American and 85% low income for the school district as a whole. Eight percent of students impacted by school closings were homeless, while students experiencing homelessness constituted around 4% of CPS's overall student population (CEFTF, 2014).

HOMELESS EDUCATION POLICY: MCKINNEY–VENTO

I do not really think that people have thought about using the McKinney–Vento Act as an opportunity to specifically speak about racial disparity. I think that the position of people who work under the act is, if we fully address the needs of these children as we want to do under this act, that, that's the turf for McKinney–Vento Homeless Education provision, Brown v. Board of Education, and etc., etc., and then the legacy of our schools with respect to racial inequality and that's a long sad story. I don't think the McKinney–Vento Act could solve that.

—Ms. Davis, McKinney–Vento advocate, July 11, 2008

Schools that serve K–12 students ideally provide the needed tools to assist in the academic and social development of children and youth, preparing all children and youth to succeed in higher education and/or vocational settings. When children and youth become homeless, keeping up with their role as students becomes difficult (Murphy & Tobin, 2011). In response to these growing concerns, the U.S. Congress passed the Stewart B. McKinney Homeless Assistance Act (1987), now referred to as McKinney–Vento in accordance with revisions under the No Child Left Behind Act (NCLB). Subsection "Part B—Education for Homeless Children and Youth," which provides federal and state funding, mandates certain actions by any state that agrees to accept funding under the Act (Heybach, 2000). The impetus for the subsection of McKinney–Vento was reports that over 50% of homeless children and youth were not attending school regularly (National Center for Homeless Education, 1999). This was reflected in the experiences of Michael, a sophomore at Grand High, and John, a freshman at Diversey High; both consistently missed school days and/or arrived to school halfway through the school day. John explained, "My grades dropped because I had missed school . . . and I haven't had the time to do all the make-up work."

Barriers to enrollment and educational access present a major obstacle to academic progress for homeless children and youth (National Coalition for the Homeless [NCH], 2005). The McKinney–Vento Act is a comprehensive act that includes funding appropriation (although not sufficient) for a wide array of services such as food, shelter, and medical care. Prior to the 1987 McKinney Act, there were practically no standards (federal, state, or local) to address the educational rights and needs of homeless children and youth within schools. Homelessness as defined under McKinney–Vento includes individuals who lack a fixed, regular, and adequate nighttime residence. Of particular significance to this work is the defining of unaccompanied youth—those not in the consistent care of a parent or legal guardian (NCLB/McKinney–Vento, 2002).

During the 1980s key advocates, political actors, and some sectors of the general public understood and conveyed that homelessness was not the responsibility of homeless individuals themselves, but instead was a reflection of a larger systemic problem, and some proposed solutions began to mirror this line of thinking. However, a long struggle ensued prior to the passage of homeless policy, and continues today, to address the myriad of issues connected to and contributing to homelessness in the United States. McKinney–Vento was meant to be a "first step" in addressing the issue of homelessness (NCH, 2006). Yet even that first step, while proscribed, has had limited success.

Preceding McKinney–Vento, children and youth were denied entrance into schools if they lacked such things as proof of permanent residence, medical records, social security cards, and so forth. The McKinney–Vento Act mandates that all children and youth be enrolled in schools immediately without having the required documentation, to reduce the number of school days children may miss. Despite the implementation of this act, there is a high mobility rate associated with homelessness, having severe educational consequences. It has been over 20 years since McKinney–Vento was first signed into law, yet many homeless students are still denied access to, and enrollment in, schools due to their status as homeless and based on their inability to provide records (e.g., furnishing a permanent address, immunization records), in direct disregard of the law.

The McKinney–Vento Act, as statutory law, addresses the majority of barriers and issues frequently encountered by families, children, and youth experiencing housing instability; therefore, it is rational that most legislative efforts focus on its implementation. Considerable research and literature on educational policy for students experiencing homelessness concentrates efforts on monitoring compliance and identifying violations committed by districts and schools that do not properly implement McKinney–Vento (Biggar, 2001; Da Costa Nunez & Collignon, 1999; Heybach, 2000; Mawhinney-Rhoades & Stahler, 2006). Where most would agree that proper implementation is an issue, the problem that still deserves our attention are the social barriers to education (such as racism and classism) that homeless students continue to endure. Specific reasons for lack of implementation named in the literature include lack of awareness; lack of funding; poor dissemination of information; lack of coordination with districts, school staff, and local agencies serving homeless students; and lack of accountability at local, state, and federal levels (Biggar, 2001; Markward, 1994; U.S. Department of Education, 2002; see Murphy & Tobin, 2011, for additional discussion of these issues). Further, Miller (2013) notes, "These [policy outcomes] however, do not appear to be uniformly distributed throughout the United States as a host of contextual factors complicate the policy's full implementation" (p. 829). Understanding the experiences of unstably housed students by considering contextual factors of race, specifically in the hypersegregated context of Chicago, will contribute to understanding the ineffectual McKinney–Vento implementation for a large subset of the homeless student population. The McKinney–Vento Act was meant to be a "first-step" in addressing homelessness; however, even if this law were fully enforced in schools, it is simply not enough to address the symptoms or causes of homelessness. States need to be more proactive in its prevention. Simultaneously addressing the hierarchical racial and class systems that perpetuate poverty and homelessness will promote an examination of its root causes and, ideally, more adequate solutions. The relationship between McKinney–Vento policy, institutional structures, and their influence on unstably housed students of color is the focus of this book.

SOCIAL CONTEXT OF HOMELESSNESS

The exceptions prove the rule. The dominant narrative can
then point to all the social programs in place as evidence of the
generosity of the successful toward those who, with effort, could
rise up. Programs, however, are meant to assist those struggling,
not to *alter the structures that cause struggle.* . . . However, in
the bootstraps ideology, there is a denial of such structures and a
belief that the individual homeless person could, with the helping
hand of the well-off, get herself off the street, into a job and into a
successful life.

—Sabina E. Vaught, *Racism, Public Schooling, and the
Entrenchment of White Supremacy*

People of color represent almost 60% of the U.S. population experiencing homelessness (U.S. Department of Housing and Urban Development,
2010), and, at the time of this research, 87% of students experiencing
instability (read: homelessness) in Chicago Public Schools were African
American, illuminating an overrepresentation of African American students, as they made up 50% of the CPS student body (CPS, 2008).

Consequently, in looking at the needs and the poor support of homeless students, it is important to keep in view the interplay between race
and class (in addition to other positionalities) as it pertains to the systems
and structures that shape the experiences of unstably housed students. A
great challenge of identifying unstably housed students is the term used
to label them: *homeless.* The general understanding of homelessness con-
jures up images of adult men and women living in parks or under bridges
and panhandling on freeway ramps or in other public spaces. In reality,
approximately 1.6 million children and youth (Murphy & Tobin, 2011)
make up the population of individuals experiencing housing instability.
While *homelessness* is the term primarily used to describe students experiencing instability, the terms *homeless(ness)*, *unstably housed*, and *instability* will be used interchangeably in an effort to both honor and complicate
the experiences and terminology widely accepted and understood in policy, community, and school settings.

Homeless youth are a medically at-risk and underserved population
in the U.S. (Ensign, 2004). They are also at great risk for physical abuse,
injuries, homicide, and suicide (Institute for Children, Poverty and Homelessness [ICPH], 2013; Murphy & Tobin, 2011); approximately 5,000

per year die from illness, suicide, and assault (Klein et al., 2000). While some of the data on homeless youth are older, nothing in our economic–racial culture or our school treatment of related problems suggests that these data would be any better today; in fact, they would likely be worse. Common health problems identified by homeless youth include human immunodeficiency virus (HIV)/acquired immunodeficiency syndrome (AIDS), sexually transmitted diseases (STDs), pregnancy, malnutrition, injuries, and dermatologic problems (Ensign & Gittelson, 1998; ICPH, 2013; Murphy & Tobin, 2011). Homeless youth have significantly greater obstacles blocking their access to health care than all other age groups, despite being at greater risk for illness (Klein et al., 2000). Youth who are consistently able to access health care are often not afforded the opportunity to speak with their health care provider privately to discuss sensitive issues such as pregnancy, HIV/AIDS, and STDs (Ensign & Gittelsohn, 1998; ICPH, 2013). Homeless youth often rely on emergency rooms for their health care needs, due to their lack of knowledge and ability to access regular health care. Emergency rooms are often their only access to care due to lack of insurance, confidentiality, and embarrassment at their status as homeless youth (American Academy of Pediatrics [AAP], 1996; ICPH, 2013; Klein et al., 2000). Despite youth's increased risk for illness and injury, they are less likely to seek out care due to their mistrust of adults (Klein et al., 2000). This was the case for many of the unstably housed youth encountered at Grand and Diversey, the high schools studied in depth as the basis for this book. One particular student, Leon, a sophomore at Grand High, had special education needs due to a learning disability as well as struggles with mental health. His lack of access to consistent, stable housing placed him at risk for both medical and emotional health needs due to inclement weather and stress from family conflict and his unstable housing status. He would often sleep in apartment hallways or abandoned buildings, neither dwelling providing sufficient heat and/or security. As a result, during the school year Leon accessed the emergency room due to his health needs; he was also placed in a mental health facility during a school break at the recommendation of the school social worker and school psychologist.

As in Leon's case, research indicates that homeless youth are more likely to demonstrate high rates of mental health problems—behavioral problems, depression, anxiety, and self-harm (ICPH, 2013; Vostanis, Grattan, & Cumella, 1998). *Mental health problems* can be defined as behavioral and emotional difficulties causing concern or distress. Rates of mental health problems are high among homeless children and youth in the United States (ICPH, 2013). Violence in the home and mental ill-ness among parents are identified as risk factors both for youth home-lessness and mental illness among the homeless youth population (ICPH, 2013; Vostanis, 1999). Data on homeless youth indicates high rates of depression, substance abuse, mental illness, and suicide attempts (AAP, 1996; Ensign & Gittelson, 1998; ICPH, 2013). Mental health is often not viewed as a "serious" problem, unlike the perception of the seriousness of physical health (Aviles & Helfrich, 2004). The complexity of issues home-less youth face (e.g., abuse and involvement in the child welfare system) is related to underlying psychosocial factors (Vostanis et al., 1998). Men-tal health problems have a negative stigma attached to them; therefore, homeless youth are less likely to seek out mental health services (Reid, 1999). Additionally, youth often self-medicate with street drugs, rather than attempting to obtain needed mental health services (Reid, 1999). This is of particular importance in Chicago as public mental health ser-vices and centers have significantly declined; 6 of 12 public mental health clinics have been closed (Joravsky, 2013).

Another student, Sheila, an 18-year-old African American female in her senior year at Grand High, shared that she left her parents' home at the end of her junior year after an argument with her stepfather. By Shei-la's report, her stepfather is an abusive man, who physically and emotion-ally abused her, her mother, and siblings. Sheila has dealt with emotional and physical abuse for many years, and the last time her stepfather was physically abusive toward her, she decided she would no longer allow him to treat her this way and demonstrated this resistance by leaving home. Sheila explained,

> So we were going to go to church and he got upset with me, 'cause
> he has this thing where we have to say good morning to him every
> morning and that morning, I didn't see him because I usually stay
> in my room and when it was time to go, my brother and sister had
> already said good morning to him. He was upset with me, because I
> didn't say good morning to him. So he chose to grab me by my neck
> and threaten me and ask me like why didn't I say good morning to
> him, and I guess I just got upset with that, and I told myself that
> that was the last time he was gonna EVER do anything to me. So
> basically I called my aunt and I told her what was going on and
> I told my mother that I wasn't going to get in the car with him
> because he was going to take us to church. Everybody was out in
> the car, my sister, my brother, my mother was trying to persuade me

to come, he was in the car, he came back in the house and asked my mother what was the problem, then he thought that he could just put his hands on me again and pull me and push me all around the house and ya know, so I just didn't like that. So that was when I sat down on the couch and I was waiting on my auntie to get there, and he said that you walk out of here with what you have on your back and don't look back. And he didn't let me get my clothes, my shoes, none of that. He just let me go with nothing and I really had no way to get my clothes or anything. I had to basically start all over, and try to work my way up myself.

As a result of this dynamic, Sheila's housing situation has become unstable; she has been staying with her grandmother, cousin, aunt, and aunt's boyfriend in the home they all share.

According to the McKinney–Vento Act, the term *homeless children and youths* includes "children and youths who are sharing the housing of other persons due to loss of housing, economic hardship, or a similar reason . . . due to the lack of alternative adequate accommodations" (No Child Left Behind Act, 2002, Section 725(2)(B)(i)).

While some would argue that Sheila is not homeless, due to her access to a "home," Sheila's departure from her parents' household places her in an unstable situation, both physically (no access to her home of origin) and emotionally (no access to support from her parents and siblings). As a result, she is not in the consistent care of a parent or legal guardian. While she is currently housed with family, Sheila clarifies, "Living with my mom felt more like a home, more of a family interaction . . . in my current household, we don't talk, everybody is just like isolated, go in our rooms and close the doors type of thing." Understanding that homelessness has meaning and implications beyond access to housing is critical to recognizing the precariousness of the situations that unstably housed youth face. Sheila is recognized as homeless under McKinney–Vento and as a result receives selected services (e.g., transportation, free breakfast/ lunch) to support her access and engagement with school. As we continued our discussion, it became apparent that the school structures and support instigated by McKinney–Vento were simultaneously beneficial and limited in their ability to fully address the complex needs that unstably housed students require and have a right to when navigating educational institutions. As Sheila traverses these structures, it is important to recognize the multiple positions she occupies, including the social constructs of race, class, gender, sexuality, and so forth that influence the manner in which educational institutions perceive and treat her. This is of increased significance when the vast majority of unstably housed students in CPS are students of color.

The myriad of challenges created by educational institutions and experienced by homeless youth distorts our understanding of their capabilities. Unaccompanied homeless youth of color (as well as other homeless children and youth) possess great talents, strengths, and resiliency. This was evident in the choices and problem solving that the youth I interacted with demonstrated as they accessed education, support, and guidance from their respective schools and various social networks. Countering the deficit narrative associated with youth experiencing instability, this work will also highlight the tenacity of unaccompanied homeless youth of color as they sought to attain stability and consistency in their lives. I can only guess how many of these youth would have succeeded if provided the minimal societal and educational support that equity and our laws demand, and what these numbers of grit-tested and well-educated young people might have contributed and be contributing right now.

THE NEXUS OF INSTITUTIONAL RACISM, CLASSISM, AND EDUCATION

Close examination of educational systems across the nation reveal that black and Latino students are more segregated now than two decades ago, the schools they attend are comparatively under resourced, and within the schools they are provided fewer academic opportunities and are treated more punitively than their white counterparts.

—Karen Fulbright-Anderson, Keith Lawrence,
Stacey Sutton, Gretchen Susi, and Anne Kubisch,
Structural Racism and Youth Development

While some researchers note that homelessness reflects issues of class, not those of race (Liebow, 1993; Wilson, 1987), recognizing that African Americans and Latinas/os are disproportionately represented among the homeless population in large urban cities such as Chicago challenges our understanding of the ways in which their status as students of color impacts the manner in which educational institutions regard this particular population of unstably housed students. Mills (2003) asserts, "With the shift from explicitly racist public discourse to the more sanitized language of the post–Civil Rights Act struggles . . . Left critics see the 'underclass' as the latest entry in this old semantic shell game, a way of talking about blacks (and increasingly, Latinos) without talking about blacks" (p. 125). Further, Soss, Fording, and Schram (2011) state, "In poverty governance today, racial biases are not driven primarily by individuals who are conscious racists. They mostly arise 'behind the backs' of officials whose ordinary interactions and choices are structured by race in ways that (more often than not) run contrary to their own racial values" (p. 81).

As the numbers of homeless children and youth continue to rise, it is imperative for educators to examine how schools in large urban school districts are serving and meeting the needs of the homeless student population, in particular African American students as they comprise the majority of students experiencing instability in urban centers. In 2006 Illinois reported 18,624 homeless students; in 2007 this number had risen to 22,321 (CPS, 2008). During the 2007–2008 academic year there were approximately 30,000–60,000 homeless children and youth (aged birth to 21) in the state of Illinois (ISBE, personal communication, September 16, 2008). In Chicago there were 10,349 homeless students during the 2007–2008 school year (the year in which this project took place). Further, as noted earlier, 87% of the homeless student population in the Chicago Public School system was African American, although they made up 50% of the CPS student body (CPS, 2008). These numbers continue to rise. During the 2012–2013 school year ISBE reported 54,892 students experiencing instability across the state of Illinois, a 109% increase since 2009 (CCH, 2014). During the 2013–2014 school year Chicago Public Schools reported 22,144 homeless students; of these, 84.4% were African American; 12.2%, Latina/o; 1.6%, White; and 1.6%, other (Sloss & Bowhay, 2014).

The racialization process that exists in the United States permeates all social structures, policies, and daily interactions; therefore, it is critical to highlight the ways in which race plays an implicit and explicit role in McKinney–Vento policy or homeless educational policy (HEP). This discussion in no way dismisses the importance of class as integral to HEP discourse. Instead, it further complicates this analysis by contributing a lens that is inclusive of the racial components underpinning HEP. It is necessary to understand the "elliptical discourse" of a *raceclass* analysis of education, one which offers an integrated perspective of race and class (Leonardo, 2003).

Students experiencing homelessness encounter several issues and challenges; their experiences cannot be detached and therefore inevitably seep into the school context. Milner (2012) notes that "the outside of school location—where children live and the environmental conditions around them[—]can have a profound impact on students and their families. Most of these environmental situations extend far beyond the control of students and their families outside of school but shape what happens inside of it" (p. 1021). As the homeless student population continues to grow, it is essential to acknowledge students' positionality, as shaped/defined by social institutions in an effort to create school conditions that are aware of and responsive to the needs of all unstably housed students.

Tate (1997) contends that "the significance of race in the United States, and more specifically 'raced' education, could not be explained with theories of gender or class" (p. 196). Focusing solely on class assumes a "color-blind" approach to HEP implementation. According to scholars such as Bell (1973), Bonilla-Silva (2006), and Stovall (2006), a color-blind approach is in itself a "racist" act, as it fails to acknowledge the racial components embedded in society. HEP functions under the premise that all children are provided an "equal starting point." However, as Gotanda (1995) recognizes, "This metaphor ignores historical-race and cumulative disadvantages that are the starting point for so many black citizens" (p. 266). Moreover, the color-blind approach does not account for the social reality of race and racism that exist in society and the institutions that govern them. Acknowledging and theorizing race will provide a deeper understanding of the myriad of factors contributing to and perpetuating homelessness. Leonardo (2012) notes, "The coordinated but awkward dance between race and class represent the dilemma around which educators and students twirl and spin. Breaking up the dance then requires understanding what each partner contributes to racial oppression in schools" (p. 429).

The interplay between race and class were evident in both educational settings (Grand and Diversey high schools) that form the basis of this book's ethnographic underpinnings. While both Grand and Diversey high schools were functioning under similar educational structures, differences in their racial/ethnic composition also shaped the resources, access, and agency of both students and school personnel in these respective spaces. Grand High is located in a predominantly African American community, reflected in its student population (98% African American; .4% Latina/o; .2% Native American) while Diversey High is more ethnically diverse (40% African American; 40% Latina/o; 13% Asian/Pacific Islander; 5% White), also reflective of the community in which it is situated. Despite the demographic differences of Grand and Diversey high schools, both spaces had over 50 unstably housed students, primarily of African American background. For example, of the 43 students identified as homeless at Diversey High, 90%

were African American, compared to their representation of 40% of the school population. I interviewed six youth of color experiencing housing instability and five adults working to implement and oversee McKinney–Vento, providing a glimpse into the supports and challenges encountered as the youth and adults worked to understand and navigate McKinney–Vento in their respective schools and the larger CPS district.

CRITICAL RACE THEORY

I don't want to down my race, but it might seem like most Black parents may have problems, . . . like with their bodies or something, like drugs, or have failure to try to take care of their children for some reason; it could be a lot of reasons, so that could be one of the reasons why African Americans are poor.

—Sheila, unstably housed African American senior at Grand High

Race continues to be a significant factor in determining inequity in the United States (Ladson-Billings & Tate, 1995; Lynn & Dixson, 2013). Critical Race Theory (CRT) serves as a framework to help in theorizing, examining, and challenging the manner in which race and racism explicitly and implicitly impact social structures, practices, and discourses (Yosso, 2005). CRT stems from Critical Legal Studies (CLS), a movement that "challenged liberalism from the Left, denying that law was neutral, that every case had a single correct answer, and that rights were of vital importance" (Delgado & Stefancic, 2001, p. 144).

The basic tenets of CRT, as described by Delgado and Stefancic (2001), include the following features:

1. Ordinariness—racism is a normal daily occurrence in U.S. society.
2. Interest convergence—people of color only attain concessions when it is in the interests of Whites, who have the power in our hierarchical system.
3. Social constructionism—race and races are products of social thought and relations, not objective or fixed; society invents, manipulates, or retires races when convenient.
4. Differential racialization—different values are placed on different races depending on the function that dominant society (i.e., Whites) would like them to serve.

5. Intersectionality—no person has a single, unitary identity.
6. Voice-of-color—people of color are able to express unique perspectives and tell their own story.

CRT is connected to the development of a new approach to examining race, racism, and law post–civil rights movement (Tate, 1997). Although economic and housing statuses are critical to HEP, racial factors are continually ignored, specifically institutional racism under the guise of meritocracy. This color-blind approach inhibits discourse and action to address inequities that youth of color experience in addition to, or simultaneously with, their class marginalization. Framing educational access as the focal point allows race to be omitted from conversations regarding HEP for homeless youth. Rather than ignoring race, CRT places race at the center, offering a more complex discussion of the connection between poverty, homelessness, and education, which ultimately plays a role in the implementation of HEP at the school level for unstably housed students of color.

Recognizing the experiences of students of color in schools as different from their White counterparts provides a space to discuss the differences between the experiences of unstably housed students of color and the experiences of unstably housed White students. Racial values are inherent in everyday life, or as Delgado and Stefancic (2001) posit, these values are social indicators that demonstrate racial inequalities. Research demonstrates that Blacks and Latinas/os seeking housing, jobs, and loans are often rejected despite exhibiting similar qualifications to those of Whites. Blacks and Latinas/os are more likely to be imprisoned, to be living in poverty, to complete fewer years of school, and to be in more menial jobs than Whites (Delgado & Stefancic, 2001). In comparison, Whites inhabit a great majority of the "power-wielding" positions in the United States as demonstrated by the great number of Whites holding governmental and corporate positions (Winant, 2004). Whiteness is viewed as the norm (placed in the center) while all other races/ethnicities occupy space around (outside of) it. More specifically, Whiteness as the norm in many circles is known as *White privilege*. White privilege is viewed as a privileged position, a position that is rarely seen by the "holder of privilege"; characteristics of the privileged group define the social norm and often benefit from it. Lastly, members of the privileged group are able to rely on this privilege and avoid addressing other oppressed groups (Wildman & Davis, 2005).

In U.S. society Whites are often not held liable in the same manner as non-Whites. This social reality compels the question: Are unstably housed students of color held liable for their situation in the same manner as unstably housed White students? While this is not a comparative under-taking or discussion, it is critical to recognize these racial tensions and re-alities as they influence McKinney–Vento's implementation or lack thereof within schools.

While speaking with a teacher at Grand High regarding the sociopo-litical landscape in the district, she commented, "The Mayor and CEO's vision for the school district is to cater to middle-class students; there is no real concern for the current student body [poor African American students]" (fieldnotes, January 29, 2008). While the teacher's language focuses on class, given the racial composition of the school (98% Afri-can American), it is imperative that a consideration of race be explored alongside this class analysis. Several scholars have made significant con-tributions to our understanding of race in the field of education (Dixson & Rousseau, 2005; Duncan, 2005; Parker & Lynn, 2002; Solórzano & Yosso, 2002). CRT is utilized in this work to examine and analyze HEP, institutional structures, and the experiences of students and adults func-tioning within these systems, as it allows for the investigation of the social construction of race and the role it plays in McKinney–Vento implementa-tion. CRT is also used to uncover racial systems and structures that unsta-bly housed youth of color navigate daily. Ladson-Billings and Tate (1995) argue that the voice of people of color is required for a complete analysis of the educational system. Without authentic voices of people of color it is doubtful that one can say or know anything useful about education in their communities.

FROM CHARITY TO JUSTICE

When I give food to the poor, they call me a saint. When I ask why the poor have no food, they call me a communist.

—Hélder Câmara, *Dom Helder Camara: Essential Writings*

CRT requires the interrogation and challenging of the current educational structures that reify racial inequity in schools and society, specifically with regard to unstably housed students of color. The focus of CRT, and of this work, is to highlight structures that uphold these racial hierarchies and subsequent inequities. Simultaneously, as Vaught (2011) cautions, "Be-cause systems are peopled, this is a story about people. . . . I implore read-ers to withhold judgments about individual subjects and instead consider how these people are illustrative of larger systems, how they are members of cultures, some—such as Whiteness—that are in dangerous dysfunction" (p. 31). While this book tells a story about unstably housed students and their interactions with the educational system and McKinney–Vento policy, it is imperative that the choices, actions, and decisions of individuals are understood within the context of the racial, class, gender, sexuality, ability, and other hierarchies permeating U.S. society. Blaming or villainizing individuals limits needed structural and systemic analysis and change that serves to benefit the manner in which school structures respond to the educational needs of students experiencing instability and actualize McKinney–Vento in various educational contexts.

A report released by Catholic Charities USA (2008) recognized that in order to seriously address poverty in the United States, there is a need to have open and candid discussions and take actions to change the impact race has on poverty. Racism in both its individual and institutional forms deeply influences poverty while simultaneously serving as an additional barrier for people of color seeking to escape poverty. Milner (2013) critically asks, "How might racial discrimination and other forms of oppression and marginalization perpetuate homelessness?" (p. 15). In addition to understanding the ways in which racial factors perpetuate homelessness, concurrently we must ask how racial factors shape approaches taken to address homelessness, even definitions of homelessness, which in turn contributes to its maintenance.

The prevailing approach taken to address homelessness, as reflected in the erratic approach to supporting homeless students in schools, is grounded in a charitable framework. This approach is problematic due to the stigma associated with charity in which individuals (not systems) are blamed for their situations, and its inability to alter, change, or dismantle the current economic and racial hierarchy inherent in U.S. society. "The mass media contributes to the collective pejorative attitudes toward those on welfare by presenting stereotypical portrayals—often with a racial overtone—of those individuals" (Fothergill, 2003, p. 659). This framing places the blame on individuals for their situation, ignoring the systemic and structural factors inherent in the capitalist American social system. Focusing on the individual creates a value system in which society (reflective in individual attitudes and approaches) determines who is "deserving" of charitable services. Charity perpetuates an inequitable social system; "charity is produced as organizations not seeking to disturb existing political or economic arrangements" (Loseke, 1997, p. 433). If we are to truly eradicate homelessness and poverty, our efforts must focus on eliminating all forms of inequity (racial, economic, and so forth).

Charity often appeals to human emotion (Loseke, 1997); therefore, it has become common practice during the winter holidays that the general public demonstrates a "renewed" focus on aiding homeless families (e.g., food/clothing/gift drives and Salvation Army red kettle). Individuals experiencing homelessness, and certainly homeless students, experience housing insecurity throughout the year, necessitating dependable, ongoing services to address the numerous issues and needs related to their housing instability. A charitable approach was evident within both schools. While this charity springs from decent and kindhearted intentions, it is sporadic and provides inadequate support for students, masking what justice demands for them.

After a required training on McKinney–Vento at Diversey High during the month of November, several teachers approached the homeless liaison and expressed their interest in collecting money to be used to purchase gifts for students during the winter holiday. Additionally, security staff at Grand High purchased clothing for students experiencing homelessness. Charity was also implemented at the district level, as demonstrated through my conversation with the district administrator, Ms. Jones:

> A lot of it's [school supplies, uniforms] donated. . . . In the beginning of the year there's a back-to-school drive and a lot of school supplies and backpacks are donated. And then this year, we actually had some businesses do a fundraiser for our program for the uniforms, and so we ordered the uniforms and had one of the interns actually take them out [to shelters and schools]. I don't know if she's got another job now, so I'm going to have to get another intern.

A charitable approach, while offering short-term, needed help, does little to advance significant, structural changes that support effective implementation of McKinney–Vento in schools serving students experiencing instability. An approach grounded in charity to address the needs of unstably housed students leaves the failing structure intact. While donations and charity are desirable at times due to the pervasive lack of awareness and/or inadequate funding of McKinney–Vento, it is in the best interests of students experiencing housing instability that these methods be critically scrutinized, alternatively creating systems that do not rely on acts of charity. McKinney–Vento is not a charitable undertaking; it is a federal policy serving to ensure that the educational rights of students experiencing homelessness and their families are not violated. Approaching McKinney–Vento from a "rights" perspective rather than a "charitable" one reframes our understanding of the policy, simultaneously creating a strong system of accountability for individuals, schools, and districts responsible for enforcing the rights of students experiencing housing instability.

The following chapters provide a glimpse into the educational experiences of unaccompanied homeless youth of color seeking school access and educational engagement and the adults responsible for McKinney–Vento awareness and implementation within two CPS high schools, the larger CPS district, and the city of Chicago, as well as specific recommendations for areas of needed implementation and enforcement of legal protections of students' right to an education.

CHAPTER 2

Obstacles, Challenges, and Triumphs

Not a flat. Not an apartment in back. Not a man's house. Not a daddy's. A house all my own. With my porch and my pillow, my pretty purple petunias. My books and my stories. My two shoes waiting beside the bed. Nobody to shake a stick at. Nobody's garbage to pick up after.

Only a house quiet as snow, a space for myself to go, clean as paper before the poem.

—Sandra Cisneros, "A House of My Own," 1984/2004

Walking along the path leading to the main entrance of the school, I notice a flashing blue light mounted on a light pole along with a camera to monitor student activity. Adjacent to the school building are two police vehicles, a stark contrast to the large open green space. Students are lined up outside of the school doors. I join the line of students and wonder why getting into the building is taking so long. As I move with the line of students, a voice declares, "Have your ID out, book bags open, and remove any belts, watches, et cetera." Another voice calls out, "If you don't have your ID step to the right for a temporary one. You will not be allowed in the building without an ID." Moving gradually through the school doors, I can see that we are all being slowly herded toward the metal detectors mounted within 5 feet of the school's main entrance. We are further directed and sorted into groups of male and female. Security guards rustle through student book bags and personal belongings, including my own. Within minutes of being searched and screened, a bell rings indicating the start of first period. Students arriving after the start of first period are directed to the main office to purchase a temporary ID. Feeling perplexed and a bit overwhelmed by the process, I look at my watch and realize it's only 8 a.m. I wonder how students must feel having to endure this daily ritual. How does this impact their educational experiences? Further, what does this mean for students already under duress due to experiences with homelessness and instability?

JOHN

Upon entering the small office of the homeless liaison at Diversey High, I am introduced to John, a 16-year-old African American male attending one of the small schools at Diversey High. John is dressed in a white shirt and navy blue pants, reflective of the uniform policy requirement. While John is of high school age, he does not yet meet the requirements necessary to be officially in the 9th grade. As a result, he is enrolled in a program that allows him to "catch up" on his academics so that he can then be eligible to take high school courses. After successful completion of this program, John will have the opportunity to transition into Diversey High's general high school as a sophomore.

John's parents are divorced. His mother has remarried and moved out of state to be with her new husband. John and his siblings were given the option to remain with their mother and move out of state or to stay in Illinois and live with their father and various other family members and friends.

John opted to stay in Chicago, and shortly after his mother left, he moved in with his godparents. The departure of John's mother from Illinois, coupled with his conflicted relationship with his father, led to his current state of housing instability. His mother eventually returned to Illinois to live. Since her return, his mother also became homeless. She was evicted from her apartment and is now living with her brother (John's uncle). Due to this family dynamic, John and his siblings live in separate households:

> My brother was staying with my uncle, until she [mom] goes, . . .
> but the twins [siblings] are with my dad. I'm living out west with my
> mom and my uncle . . . we're homeless, but not homeless where we
> just like, living on the street. We are living with family until we can,
> uh, until my mom can get back on her feet for right now, . . . but
> I just might stay up here (near Diversey High) 'cause my school is
> close.

John has four siblings from his parent's relationship and several other siblings from their other relationships. John has minimal contact with these other siblings. However, as John is the oldest male in his family, he is often responsible for the care of his younger siblings. This responsibility directly affects his school attendance and work. While speaking with John, we are interrupted: "Excuse me John, you have a message from your mother." John steps out to call his mother. As I sit in the office, I notice a yellow and purple sign that reads "Homeless Education Program," demonstrating McKinney–Vento compliance. McKinney–Vento requires "Public notice of the educational rights of homeless children and youth is disseminated" (Illinois Education for Homeless Children Act [ILEHC], 1994). The sign outlines the criteria for homelessness and identifies the name and number of the homeless liaison at Diversey High. The homeless liaison, Ms. Franklin, working with John enters the office and shares that he often receives phone calls at school from his mother, asking him to come home to do things for her. The liaison expresses her disapproval. She states, "This is not appropriate; it has a negative impact on his ability to focus on his school work."

John's living situation is categorized as "doubled-up" as outlined in McKinney–Vento, bouncing around sleeping at various family and friends' homes, including a maternal uncle, his father's residence, and that of his godparents. Despite his instability, he has attempted to take on this responsibility for his mother and siblings:

> I still . . . it's just too much stuff I have to do in school, then I am so tired and wore out . . . when I go home, I wash up, I probably iron clothes for the next day, do homework, help my brother and them [siblings] with their homework, make sure they take their shower and iron their stuff for school. Then I might run around to the grocery store . . . because me and my momma be up runnin' around, they [siblings] call us on her cell phone and they read us the problem out of the book and we'll help them over the phone and all of that.

John's responsibilities at home and school intertwine. He has endured many hardships as a youth, including the loss of his brother to violence, as well as threats to his own safety due to violence in the communities in which both his parents live. These personal threats of violence impact his choices and options for school:

> I'm in here [small school program] because when I was in grammar school, I got in too many fights and wasn't coming to school because of safety reasons. Guns and stuff were involved . . . but we don't fight unless we have to fight, we just don't go around lookin' for a fight. I did everything I could do to get away [from previous school].

Despite these obstacles, John finds support, safety, and consistency from his godparents. There is a stark contrast between John's home life with his parents and that of his responsibilities and expectations at his godparents' home. As John states,

> My responsibilities, at home I probably like do my chores, like sweep
> and mop the kitchen floor, take out the garbage, clean my room
> if it's messed up, uh, (pause) do the, probably do the bathroom,
> basic cleaning, and then get to homework and basically the same
> thing. . . . But at my godparents' house, all I got to do when I walk
> through the door, is get straight to my homework, and show them
> my homework and they check it. Oh we can't play video games on
> weekdays. They want us on top of our work, stay focused, but we
> can be on the computers, they don't take that away from us, we can
> play games on the computers. All our responsibilities are marked on
> the calendar, like if I'm washing dishes, my [god]brother will have to
> do the garbage, take out the garbage and sweep and mop the floor.

Due to the instability of John's parents, they are currently unable to provide him with the consistency he requires to focus on himself and his education. Although John lacks consistency and stability from his biological parents, he reports receiving support and guidance from his godparents and adults at school. John shares his thoughts about school staff he deems helpful and supportive:

> Sweet, kind, they always be there when you're down or need help, or
> if something's troubling, bothering you, you can always come to one
> of your teachers to talk to them, so you tell them about what's going
> on, 'cause you know sometimes you can't talk to your mom and dad
> about it, then you'll have to come and talk to them [teachers] and
> they'll understand what I'm going through and all that.

He continues:

> Well, they [teachers] ask me what's going on, I tell friends, I know the
> lunchroom people, teachers, most of the teachers. I don't know all
> the teachers through the whole building, but teachers I know they ask
> me where I've been, am I ok, why I ain't comin' to school. They're
> concerned about me and I let them know I'm alright, that I'm going
> through some family things, problems, and people tryin' to get at me
> and you can't let that go on. Really you know sometimes my mom

be getting into a lot trouble, and I have to be there so, I don't want nothing to happen to my mom, and it just be so much, so when it's all over, after all the fighting and stuff, I still have to do homework, iron my clothes for tomorrow, take a shower that day, and I'm done at like almost one in the morning, I gotta get up at like five in the morning, I be sleepy.

When John was asked about challenges he currently faces, he responded:

Fighting, fighting a lot. Fighting against other family, or gangbangers on the streets that just be knowin' the neighborhood, and what comes up to the neighborhood, that kind of sort of thing. Once you show them you ain't on that, or you ain't trying to fight, like we just moved around here, now you all trying to fight and we fight you all, now they trying to shoot at us and stuff, I be gettin' tired of fighting all the time, I want to do something else than fight, but shoo, the world messed up, everywhere you go, you got some kind of trouble.

The conflict John experiences at home seeps into his academic life. The stresses of family life and community violence interrupt his academic pursuits.

Lastly, John adds:

Being in school is a big, big thing for me because school, like say for instance if I wanted to get to the NBA, my momma couldn't do it, my father couldn't do it, my school can help me, but I gotta keep them good grades up, keep doing what I'm doing, and I can do like a year or two of college. And when I do get there, there's a lot of things to do: buy my mom her own house, her own barbershop cause she likes to do hair, make sure my brothers and sisters are alright.

John's experiences with school staff and his perception of school is indicative of his belief in the power of education. His belief in school personnel and their subsequent support of John illustrate the critical role schools can serve in facilitating his academic goals. Schools can function as an anchor of stability and support, enhancing students' ability to engage in their education.

Although John does not have an understanding of McKinney–Vento legislation, he is able to articulate the services he receives as a student experiencing instability, which include free breakfast and lunch and transportation. Outside of these services John could not identify other formal services. When asked about his awareness of rights, John replied:

> Like if we homeless . . . we get, they give us bus cards and stuff, to get back and forth to school, um not that we trying to get around our school fees, basically we struggling and need help . . .

Asked to look over the homeless students educational rights form (see Appendix B) and see if other listed services would be helpful, he looks it over and offers:

> Yeah. Probably enrollment, participate; remain, and um obtain.

When "remain and obtain" were explained to mean being able to remain in your school, being able to participate in support programs and then being able to get information about all the different waivers that you should have access to, John said he would like to have a copy of the list of rights and services. John's lack of awareness of his rights speaks to an important area in which McKinney–Vento is not being implemented well. As a student, he cannot ensure his rights are being met if he is not aware of those rights. According to McKinney–Vento, it is the responsibility of the school via the homeless liaison to make sure students are aware of their rights to various services and support that are meant to facilitate educational access and success. While there were signs posted regarding the criteria for homelessness and the contact information for the school's liaison, students were not fully informed of their rights. Within Diversey High, informing students of their rights and optional services is very much the exception, not the rule.

As John shares his experiences, he also reflects on his understanding of the meaning of *homelessness*:

> The meaning of the word *homeless* its just like shoo, things going real bad for us so we gotta put people, to put some of our brothers and sisters here and there cause we, til my momma can find her a job and we can get back on our feet, get us a house or apartment or something just all our, staying with another relative, so they could help us out til we find an apartment or a building, which we homeless, but we not homeless. . . . Uh, probably they [person experiencing homelessness] was going through some things and they needed help, and they couldn't do it on their own, or they sometimes probably the father wasn't there, and the mother cannot support

a family on her own. And the kids try to do everything they could but they also gotta come to school and all that, so and probably the mother can't do everything and she probably lose her apartment, and they become homeless and they probably have to move to a shelter and all that, it's just sad.

John's perception reflects his personal experience with instability, noting a single mother trying her best to provide for her family, and the child's (John's) attempts to support his mother. John's story is also rooted in a racialized experience. African American families, and youth in particular, are overrepresented among persons living in poverty and experiencing homelessness. "The finding that blacks are overrepresented in [homeless] shelter[s] when compared to whites demonstrates that blacks continue to face prejudice and substantial access barriers to decent employment, education, health care, and housing not experienced by whites" (Da Costa Nunez, Adams, & Simonsen-Meehan, 2012, p. 3).

Additionally, the violence John describes is prevalent in poor communities of color, specifically African American communities in Chicago and other urban contexts. Further, school staffs are familiar with John's situation. In the larger school and social contexts, many young Black boys are victims and perpetrators of violence and are often at an academic disadvantage in comparison to their White counterparts. Due to the social construction of race, John's experience with instability and violence are perceived as a normal part of his day-to-day living. He accepts this reality with little to no resistance or critique of the social forces, structures, and dynamics that create and perpetuate hierarchies of race and class.

NATALIE

While I was sitting in the main office of Diversey High, Natalie, a 16-year-old African American sophomore entered. Natalie is a "typical" teenage girl in the sense that she is very fashion conscious, always sure her hair and makeup are done, and often adorns herself with multiple bracelets on both wrists; necklaces, both short and long, hang around her neck. Natalie is visibly upset and asks to speak with Mr. Riley, the homeless liaison. Early in the school year, Natalie's mother went to Barbados to help care for her mother (Natalie's grandmother), who was ill. While there, Natalie's mother was involved in an accident, leaving her with injuries that did not allow her to travel back to the States temporarily. As a result Natalie has been under the care and supervision of her stepdad. Their relationship is tumultuous, leaving Natalie feeling hurt and alone. Natalie left her home after an argument with her stepdad in which the police were called. Natalie feared that her stepdad would physically hurt her and saw calling the police as a solution to her problem:

> On Sunday, they [stepdad and brother] tried to talk tough and stuff like so I called the police, because he looked like he wanted to hit me, he was like wait to you get out the bathroom you know . . . people keep on turning on me, and they would look at me like, the police, that day when the police came to the apartment, they'll listen to my dad, like I ain't got no say in it and stuff all like that.

Since that incident, their relationship has taken a downward turn, with Natalie continually leaving home to seek out refuge from the conflict occurring at home. She is seeking support from Mr. Riley to find housing. Mr. Riley recalls that I previously worked with a youth shelter and hopes that I can assist with Natalie's situation. We call a local youth shelter and fortunately there is a bed available for Natalie. She speaks to the intake person and is informed they will hold the bed until 8 p.m. Natalie's hands are shaking. "I don't know how to get to the shelter, how will I get there?" Mr. Riley provides her with fare cards to get to the youth shelter and to return to school the following day along with directions. "What is the shelter like?" Natalie asks. I provide her with a description of the shelter and the day-to-day routine. Natalie sighs, "OK, sounds like it will be better than home." Sitting up a bit, she exclaims, "I have to go home first and get my belongings, I hope he [stepfather] is not there!" The fear of an encounter with her stepfather overwhelms Natalie. Recognizing Natalie's anxiety, Mr. Riley and I talk with her a bit more. We hope this will alleviate her nervousness. I also recognize the real safety concern Natalie has. What if he is home and is upset by her plan to leave? This poses a real threat for Natalie. While we have identified a "safe" space for her, she may be subjected to physical violence in order to get there. How does a 16-year-old process these feelings of violence and safety? Do the risks outweigh the benefits?

In addition to recognizing these safety concerns, I couldn't help but wonder what the solution would have been in my absence. Homeless liaisons are provided with a handbook that should serve to guide their work. There are several shelters listed in the appendixes of the *Homeless Education Program Manual*. However, as illustrated here, the homeless liaison was not equipped and/or trained to assist Natalie with securing housing, resulting in a direct violation of McKinney–Vento. According to the Illinois State Board of Education (2013) *Policy of the Illinois State Board of Education on the Education of Homeless Children and Youth Overview* document, "School districts should develop relationships, and coordinate, with agencies providing services to the families of homeless children and youth" (p. 6). Further, beyond this logistical matter, neither of us was really able to alleviate Natalie's concerns. The perceived threat of violence was palpable. Truly, we were limited in ensuring her safe passage from home to shelter. Thankfully, Natalie was able to obtain some belongings, arrive safely at the shelter, and return to school the following day.

Natalie was born and lived in Barbados with her grandmother until 4 years ago, when her mother decided it was time for Natalie to come live with her and her husband in Chicago. Natalie does not have contact with her biological father and met her stepfather for the first time when she moved to the States. Natalie explains:

> My mom was dating my stepdad, he left my mom to come over here, so he meet a different woman, so my mom move on and she had me with a different man; but she had my two brothers with that man before me. But they left like in 2000 to come here, so they don't really know me since I grew up, ya know, yeah, they left when I was still young.

Prior to Natalie's coming to the United States, her mother would visit Barbados a few times a year to spend time with her. Natalie's adjustment to living in the United States with her mother and stepfather has not been an easy one. Natalie's struggle to fit in with her peers has resulted in conflict with her stepfather and, ultimately, her current homeless situation:

> I cannot have no friends, I mean I know what they [friends] did was wrong, to come in my home and drink. That's why I don't talk to my friends no more ya know, but I wasn't drinking. You can take me, bring me, and see if I was drinking or not, but ya know he could talk to me like "you shouldn't do that," ya know. He just gonna start disrespecting me and stuff like that, bring my big brother into this ya know, he probably want to hit me or something . . . so I had to call the police, and they like you should get out. So that's why I told my counselor, and she's looking for a place I could go.

In addition to this conflict, Natalie feels that her mother is not understanding, caring, or supportive of her:

She, she don't talk to me ya know, your child come home from
school, she don't like, "how was your day?" and ya know, "what
did you do today at school?" and like I think she should ya know.
Like I come in [from school], it's like I'm not there, I'm transparent,
like you could look through me and you can't see nothing, and
you could just look right through me and that's it, ya know. Your
daughter come home and you not like "what did you do today" and
"show me your work" and stuff like that, nothing; they just like, I'm
not even there, that's how they treat me.

Natalie feels as though she is not heard and is missing out on her emotional needs, feeling "transparent" to her mom, suggesting her desire for
adult care and support. Our conversation about her relationship with her
mom takes an unexpected turn toward race:

And I think my mom she act like, she don't. . . . Probably in
Barbados, they act tough and stuff like that, ya know she's different.
I wish I had a White mom, ya know.
    'Cause they soft and nice, ya know they pick you up from
school, they talk to you, sometimes I see White people with they kids
ya know, they so nice. A Black person like, oh whatever, you my
daughter, whatever, they don't care, like I don't a have a special type
like moms do, yeah, but majority of like Black person, you never
see them having a nice conversation with they kid so they think you
Black, so you probably tough. A White person, ya know they talk to
they kids and ya know, comfort them; a Black person wouldn't do
that.

Asked if this is what she sees in her experience of friends at school,
Natalie responds:

Yeah, I got a friend, and her mom, she's like White and her mom
is nice, sometimes like she talk stuff; and I'm like you better stop
because your mom is too nice, she buy her stuff, she take care of
her, she will call her like 24/7 of the day, "Are you OK girl?" and
I listen to their conversation. My mom would never do that, never
in her life do that. I'm telling you, (becoming emotional) I see some
kids sometimes and they're like, "I don't want to go home because
my mom doesn't want to let me go to the movies"; I'm like that's so
stupid, you have the world's greatest mom, and you don't want to go

home 'cause your mom don't want to take you to the movies. That's a stupid reason you know. Mine is so complicated like, I don't know why my life gotta be so hard and difficult, it's just not fair.

Natalie's sentiment regarding Black and White parents speaks to the reification of racial perceptions, characteristics, and hierarchies held by society at large, as well as her perceptions of herself and other Black women. CRT allows for the recognition that Natalie's racial understandings are an outcome of the racial hierarchy embedded in social institutions that places Whites over all racial/ethnic persons. Research demonstrates that Black and White adolescents experience family conflict at similar rates. According to Hammer et al. (2002), there is no particular racial/ethnic group that is disproportionately represented among youth experiencing family conflict. They give the following statistics for youth aged 7–17: White youth—57% of runaways/thrownaways and 66% of the general U.S. population; Black youth—17% of runaways/thrownaways, 15% of the general U.S. population; and Hispanic/Latina/o youth—15% of runaways/thrownaways, 14% of the U.S. population. This reality contradicts the perception held by Natalie that White parents are "nice and soft" in comparison to their Black counterparts.

Natalie's lack of home support prompted her to seek out assistance from her school counselor, who referred her to the homeless liaison at Diversey High. Natalie's actions are a reflection of her resilience and faith in the school system to support her. As Natalie moves from shelter to home, she expresses many concerns regarding basic needs such as food and clothing. She also shares that her relationship with her stepdad is not consistent, and this has only made her home situation worse:

I'll say "afternoon" and he kiss his teeth like this (makes a "smacking" sound with her mouth). And I go to my room, or sometime he say "hi" to me, and I go in, sometimes he doesn't answer me; I don't care, ya know. I just go in my room . . . I closed up my room door so, then I come to school the next morning. My stepdad, didn't give me no lunch money, nothing, ya know I haven't eaten, no dinner in like a week now. After I come to school I go home, lock up my room door, and watch TV.

The strained relationship coupled with inconsistent parental care makes it difficult for Natalie to focus in school, as she does not know what she will face every time she returns home.

Students' inability to identify a person or persons of support often leaves them feeling isolated and overwhelmed. Natalie describes the manner in which this negatively impacts her school engagement and success:

> It's the whole thing, like I been through a homeless shelter and all
> of that stuff, and some nights I don't eat and I just ya know I got a
> different appetite for certain stuff. I don't want to come to school,
> like my life like changed from that moment this man started arguing
> with me, I don't know. Last year I had honors English, good stuff,
> but now I don't want to come to school, my grades are going
> down. . . . It's making me like I can't learn, 'cause I got a lot of stuff
> going on in my head, instead of like, look you got your child, you
> should make like she's good and even once a week have a talk with
> your child, like you know make sure their brain is good. It's like
> I got so many stuff going on in my head like, so many things I'm
> thinking about, my learning part can't function.

Natalie's words show a very deep intuitive but neurologically accurate understanding of how life stresses can make learning nearly impossible (Ashdown & Bernard, 2012). Natalie is a student who received little support at home or school. She consistently argued with her stepfather and believed that her mother sided more with him than her. This student recognizes the impact of housing instability on her academic ability and outcomes. Her experiences with homelessness influenced her emotional and cognitive development and overall functioning. The stress Natalie was under due to her experience with homelessness also impacted her mental health, making it difficult to meaningfully engage and learn in her classes.

Further, Natalie shares that many of her teachers were not sensitive to her unstable situation:

> Sometimes I swipe in [to school], I don't know why I do it,
> sometimes. I'm coming with like an intention of going to class and
> then you going to hear people talking about it like "why were you
> not here?" and this teacher says this and I just leave, once I hear they
> start talking to me about this stuff, I just leave.

Natalie gets discouraged by the constant questions about where she has been, why she hasn't come to class:

> This teacher say, "you not here and I called the social service
> agency," ya know my division teacher, she'll come to me and say,

and some of my teachers, like I try to get you and they like, you in a shelter, I try to call the social service agency, right in front of the class.

She feels (rightly so) that the teachers don't respect her privacy:

Once they see me, like if I'm in the hallway with a bunch of kids, they like, "I tried to call you and your number went to a shelter," right in front of a bunch of kids.

This highly insensitive lack of understanding by her teachers, coupled with violations of Natalie's privacy as outlined in McKinney–Vento, speaks to the limited reach legislation can have in practice. It also highlights the lack of understanding some teachers may have regarding the feelings and perceptions of students experiencing housing instability.

The turmoil Natalie experienced at home led to her decision to leave her parents' residence. However, her willingness to return home and attempt to engage her stepfather reflects a nuanced experience of instability. Although Natalie expresses her frustration and anger toward her stepfather and mother, she shares the following regarding what schools can do to help students in her situation:

They [school personnel] could probably, they could have a parent conference, and let your kids, like write down some stuff that's bothering them at home, and then they show it to the parents, and the parents try to make amends with the kid. They tell them oh, I'm not going to do that or stuff like that, or if that can't work out, find a place to put the kids I guess. But at least they should like have a conference, like the kids write down what's bothering them and they show their mom and stuff, ya know and try to help.

Blackman (1998) found that many homeless youth have experienced years of not being heard or listened to at home or in school. Natalie's desire to be reunited with her mother and to have a space in which she can better express herself in an effort to communicate with her mother contradicts popular beliefs about youth experiencing instability. It also exemplifies the creativity, sincerity, and resiliency of youth in attempting to address and resolve family conflict.

Additionally, Natalie has been speaking with a counselor from a local social service agency that provides services to "at-risk" youth. She shared the following:

She like, she talk to me and ask me like what's been going on at home and like, she supposed to give me a home and stuff like that, but it seems like that's taking forever, 'cause she told me that it's going to take 2 months and its been like more than 2 months yeah. So, that probably ain't going to happen right now.

The counselor doesn't inquire much about Natalie's home situation. As Natalie sees it, the counselor meets briefly with many students, basically checking in but not providing much assistance or even enough time to really talk:

She's like the counselor for the homeless kids that come to Diversey High, which is a lot, so you know when I get my turn with her, it's not long, so I can tell her my situation and stuff like that, it's like a short time: "Hello, how are you?" "What's going on?" and "Bye."

As expressed by Natalie, very little time and seemingly little will is provided to significantly address the myriad of issues she currently faces. Natalie's commentary demonstrates the limited time and superficial approach nonteaching staff bring to a much needed service to youth experiencing housing instability. The long wait time (2 months promised and even this promise not met) in finding a suitable housing placement for Natalie highlights the lack of housing options available to serve the needs of youth experiencing instability, reflecting a larger systemic issue. In Chicago there are only 20 designated Permanent Supportive Housing units that are provided by just two Chicago-area nonprofits (Aviles de Bradley & Holcomb, 2014).

The notion of caring is important for all youth. For Natalie, this is of particular importance, and she describes the kind of interaction she would like to have with staff:

Yeah, yeah, you know you could ask or be my friend, like "Hey Natalie, come to school man," ya know, and try to help me, "You could like stop by in my office, we could have lunch, and we can talk about some stuff."

In other words, they could care more:

They should have, they should let the student know that homeless is not a bad stuff and stop judging the next kid, ya know, if you see a girl in like dirty pants, you know, just come on, that's just pants, don't judge that person, if you come up here wearing dirty shoes, before they even look at your face, you know they going to talk about your clothes. What's that?

Natalie finds this behavior characteristic of students as well as teachers.

The notion of caring is particularly critical for youth in a homeless situation. Often, they do not have access to a consistent caring adult outside of the school context. Research finds that a nurturing relationship with a trusted adult has a positive impact on healthy development (Elster, 2008). Once again, schools become vital spaces in which students can be engaged, supported, and cared for through interactions with school staff and personnel.

Natalie's attendance became very sporadic as the school year progressed. On one occasion, Natalie and I were to meet during her lunch period. I had seen her swiping in earlier that morning; however, she was not at lunch. As I scanned the lunchroom to try and find her, a security guard approached me. "Who are you looking for?" he inquired. I replied, "Natalie Davis." "I haven't seen her today, try again tomorrow" was his reply. While I was surprised that he knew her by name, I didn't think much of it. A couple of weeks later, I was able to catch up with Natalie. We talked about her spotty attendance and the many causes for it. Despite these obstacles, Natalie identified folks in the school building that she felt supported her:

Yeah, like Thomas [security guard]. Yeah you like, he's like, where have you been? What's up with you girl, why haven't you been in school?

She values Thomas as a person who lets her know that someone cares:

And sometimes he can see when I'm having a bad day and he like, what's wrong? Even Ms. Black [security guard], she do that too. . . . The securities they good, Ms. McNair [security guard], she do that too. . . . Like ask me what's wrong and stuff like that.

As she described these interactions with security personnel, I realized that Thomas was the security guard who approached me in the lunchroom a few weeks back. On the surface, security personnel may not be the first adults we consider as "kind" and "caring," as their roles in schools are to enforce rules and ensure student safety, often through use of force. Another dimension is demonstrated by Natalie's positive interactions with the security personnel in her school, which may have implications for McKinney–Vento. While the homeless liaison is responsible for identifying and supporting students experiencing instability, ensuring all school staff, including ancillary staff, are aware of and trained on McKinney–Vento would provide much needed school level support for students. Unfortunately, the small doses of informal support Natalie received from security personnel and the homeless liaison were not enough to keep her engaged and connected to school. As she increasingly lost connections with the adults in the school, including teachers and staff, whom one would expect to provide primary encouragement and support, she stopped attending classes and eventually ceased making the effort to attend school at all.

SHEILA

"Have a seat and I'll be right back with your student," Ms. Gray declares. Within minutes, Sheila, an 18-year-old African American female in her senior year at Grand High, arrives. She is dressed in khaki pants and a light blue shirt, the required uniform for all Grand High students. Her hair is tightly braided and a silver chain adorns her neck. Sheila seems somewhat hesitant to speak with me, asking "How will this help me with college?" to which I reply "There really isn't a benefit connected to college. I would like to talk to you about your experiences with homelessness and how it affects your schooling. What you share with me will help me better understand your situation. And hopefully this information will be useful in better serving students in similar situations." Sheila sits silently. Not sure of her take on the information shared, I add, "This is not mandatory, if you aren't still interested that's OK." She asks a couple more follow-up questions and seems satisfied with my responses. After this exchange, she tells me about how she became homeless. Sheila left her parents' home at the end of her junior year, after an argument with her stepfather. Sheila discloses that her stepfather physically and emotionally abuses her and her siblings, as well as her mother (see Chapter 1 for Sheila's account of this abuse).

In addition, Sheila feels that her stepfather has been more abusive toward her than her siblings. When asked why she felt this way, Sheila replied, "I guess he just don't like the fact that I like girls," referring to her sexual identity. Although Sheila expresses her physical attraction toward girls, she does not identify as a lesbian. Sheila wishes to steer clear of being labeled as such due to the prejudice and stigma associated with the label. Many youth are "kicked out" of their homes due to issues of sexuality. Sheila recognizes that her stepfather is abusive in general; however, she feels that due to her sexual identity she receives the brunt of his abuse. Youth who identify themselves as lesbian, gay, bisexual, transgendered, or questioning (LGBTQ) are disproportionately represented among homeless youth (CCH, 2001). Between 20% and 40% of homeless youth identify as LGBTQ (Child Welfare League of America & Lambda Legal, 2012). LGBTQ individuals of all ages face a particular set of challenges, both in becoming homeless as well as when they are trying to avoid homelessness. LGBTQ youth face social stigma, discrimination, and often rejection by their families, which adds to the physical and mental strains and challenges that all homeless persons must struggle with. Frequently, homeless LGBTQ youth have great difficulty finding shelters that accept and respect them, and LGBTQ homeless youth are often at a heightened risk of violence, abuse, and exploitation compared with their heterosexual peers (Child Welfare League of America & Lambda Legal, 2012; CCH, 2001).

Currently, Sheila lives in one household with her grandmother, cousin, aunt, and aunt's boyfriend. Sheila reports that she, her mother, and siblings continue to maintain a positive relationship. This allows her to seek out support and guidance from her mother. Sheila's conflict with her stepfather has led to her current situation. When asked how her mother felt about her situation, Sheila shared:

> We never had any conversations about how I felt about anything, it was just all his word, what he say, or nothing goes. And it's just has to be that way because he says so.

The abuses Sheila and her mother endure at the hands of her stepfather have not prevented them from maintaining contact:

> I call her sometimes at work; I don't call her on her cell phone, because he like checks the bill sometimes to see what numbers are and things like that.

These "hidden" interactions have placed a strain on their relationship, making it difficult to communicate with her mother as needed. This dynamic also speaks to issues of domestic violence that often renders African American women and their children homeless. As Richie (1996) states,

Poor African American battered women in contemporary society are increasingly restricted by their gender roles, stigmatized by their racial/ethnic and class position, and constrained by the competing forces of tremendous unmet need and very limited resources. This predicament leaves them facing complicated ethical, moral, and practical dilemmas. (p. 2)

Sheila's mother may have access to such "limited resources," reducing her ability to protect Sheila and her other children. Her husband's abuse likely prohibits Sheila's mother from standing up to him, fearing for the safety of her children and herself. This racial dynamic also plays a role in Sheila's overall life experience, including her perceptions of herself, African American men, and families. When Sheila is provided with the statistic that 90% of students experiencing homelessness in CPS are African American, she replies,

I don't want to down my race, because I live around a lot of them [African Americans], but it doesn't come as a surprise to me that the amount [of African American homeless students] is so high at other schools too.

The normalcy of poverty in the lives of African American communities reifies African Americans' "place" in society. CRT allows for a space in which to interrogate these racial dynamics occurring in social structures and the larger communities comprising U.S. society. These structures result in the inequitable life outcomes for persons of color. Placing Sheila's commentary in these theoretical contexts supports her understanding and reality that African Americans overwhelmingly comprise the homeless student population of CPS. For Sheila as well as other youth who participated in this project, this racial dynamic is understood as normal, or ordinary as noted by one tenet of CRT, and therefore there is no critical reflection or discussion as to *why* society functions along these racial and class hierarchies.

Sheila's estrangement from her family has created a sense of instability in her life. This, in turn, has created a different understanding and perception of her homeless situation. Sheila differentiates her homeless situation from the more "typical" conceptions of homelessness because she lives with a grandmother:

I wouldn't say I'm homeless, because I live with family, but just not in the house that I grew up in. Homeless meaning no household, and hard to get food and things like that, hard to take care of yourself.

She thinks of "homeless people" as, "just people I see [on the street] and they ask for money, you know. If I have some change, I'll give it to them."

Sheila distinguishes her living situation from other homeless persons she comes across on the street, stating how she herself provides them with change when she is able. Her perception of these differences helps her to differentiate herself from other individuals experiencing homelessness. It also serves to perpetuate people's perceptions about homelessness in general and, more specifically, homeless individuals. This, however, may serve as a coping mechanism for her own self-image, preserving a positive outlook on how she views herself as a person and as a student. It also speaks to the need to better educate teachers, parents, and students on the evolving nature of what it means to be "homeless."

Conversely, Sheila does recognize differences between her living conditions with her grandmother versus living with her mother and stepfather. Sheila does not receive the same type or level of support from her grandmother or aunt. When asked if knowing that technically, under the law, she would be categorized as a person who doesn't have the stable household that she had before, has that changed her understanding of what homelessness means, she answers:

> It's different than living in my mother's home because, um they don't always give me money and do things; my mother, she stills gives me money when I need money and it's different. . . . And the household like, we don't talk, everybody is just like isolated, go in our room and close the doors type thing. Every now and then, ya know, we will cook dinner and sit around and talk, but it's not always though.

These housing differences have also impacted Sheila's schooling:

> I was really missing a lot of days of school because as I say, when he [stepfather] put me out, I didn't have any clothes or anything to get around anywhere, no transport, barely transportation, so that was really hard for me at the time . . . um, my grades kinda dropped. I think I got one F, that's why I'm taking Spanish right now in night school, because that was one of the, that was the only class that I failed.

Sheila's departure into homelessness and the loss of her clothes and personal things has led to instability overall, in both her home and school life.

This has led to a fracture in her sense of family and has also had a negative impact on her grades and attendance.

Attempting to garner support from her teachers, Sheila has shared with some of them her home situation. Asked why she confided in the teacher, she answered:

> Because my grade was in jeopardy for one of my classes. For my first-period class, usually when I was living with my mother, my stepfather would wake us up early, early in the morning. Um, he didn't want us taking the bus from a far distance, so he woke us up in the morning drove us to our aunt's house so that we could take one bus to school so that we would be on time. Now, um my grandmother, she doesn't wake me up, but sometimes she does, and that's why sometimes it's hard for me to be on time and being tardy and absent.

Asked how the teacher responded to what she shared, Sheila answered:

> I don't know, I'm not trying to be harsh, but he treats favoritism to certain people and I guess I had a problem with, I had him last year and I had a problem with him, and I have him again this year, and I want my class changed at the end of January, so I asked my counselor to help me with that and this year he's given me problems. He wouldn't collect my work and it just kept stacking up all my work and I went down to my counselor and I told her I have all this work and he's not collecting it, and she's like why, because I'm not on time, I mean why aren't you collecting my work, I mean it's done I did it, just because I'm not on time and I have not, just I'm mingling or doing something that I'm not supposed to be, not to be on time. It's a reason why I'm not being on time, so accept it, so it's like I have to give her my work, for her to give it to him and I guess she talked to him, and I got my work back and I gave it to him and he checked my work.

This is Sheila's first-period class, ironically Psychology, where one might expect more understanding, but that understanding was not evidenced in the teacher's interactions with Sheila.

As illustrated above, teachers may not always be understanding of a student's situation or may not make any effort to understand or make accommodation for their circumstances and may exacerbate the student's situation by being punitive. This affects students' ability to engage and participate in their education. Sheila has received much of her support by engaging in extracurricular activities and through her own motivation to seek out assistance from her counselor. In an ideal implementation of McKinney–Vento, the homeless liaison at Grand High would have time to sit with Sheila and identify with her any pressing needs that could be addressed through the school. One critical aspect of the liaison's responsibility is ensuring that students receive all services for which they are eligible (NCLB/McKinney–Vento, 2002).

Sheila's determination to remain engaged in school has benefited her educational outcomes; however, it has also resulted in her wanting reasonable support from teachers and other adults in the school.

Sheila appreciated the caring attitude of her interviewer:

> You seem concerned and I'm glad that somebody cares, so that makes me happy and it seems like somebody really cares, that matters to me but when it seems like people don't care that hurts me, a part of me inside.

Asked if at school, she feels that there's a good number of people that really care about what she's doing and where she's trying to go, she answers:

> I won't say a good number, but there's an alright number, certain people, there's not too many people, that too much really care.

She also remarks:

> Um, I think it would help students who are in school if they have therapy and someone called their parents to have them to come in, so that they can meet with them and the person who's doing the therapy. The students and their parents could all meet together, 'cause maybe they feel uncomfortable talking to their parents alone, so they want someone to question them and to talk to them, someone else to feel comfortable in the room, to make them feel comfortable so that they can talk to their parent, and this may be something going on in their life that their parent doesn't know, so it's possible that the student can get it out, having therapy with their parents sitting right there so that the parent can know and possibly do something about it and care more for their child.

Sheila's desires to have someone serve as a mediator between parent and child addresses aspects of unaccompanied homeless student need that are not specifically addressed through McKinney–Vento. This insight provides a different aspect of student need that speaks in direct contradiction to perceptions that homeless youth have no desire to mend their relationship with their parent/guardian. Similar to Natalie, Sheila expresses a wish to create a dialogue with her parents to address her emotional needs, again demonstrating a need to create structures within the school that can better address the social–emotional needs of students. In spite of the many obstacles Sheila faced (spotty attendance, drop in grades, and minimal support) she was able to successfully re-engage in her student role and graduate from Grand High by the end of the school year.

JACK

After winter break Mr. Riley comments on the increase of students identified as homeless. There were approximately 40 homeless students when the school year started, and now there are 60. The majority of these students are accompanied. However, there is a newly identified unaccompanied student, Jack. Jack is a 17-year-old African American male in the 11th grade at Diversey High. Prior to becoming homeless, Jack lived with his three siblings, his mother, and her husband. Similar to the other youth respondents, Jack has lived in poverty for many years before becoming homeless. Jack recalls that the last time he received clothing and school supplies from his mother for school was in the 7th grade. Seeking money, Jack began selling drugs with his brother while in 8th grade. Jack has been arrested several times. His most recent arrest led to his being placed on house arrest. His previous arrests have "slowed" his selling; however, the need for an income is still there, so he returns to selling drugs in order to maintain an income to buy clothes, supplies, and other items.

Currently, Jack is looking for a legal means to make money. He does not receive financial support from his mother, making it difficult to not rely on his past illegal actions to generate an income. Jack's last encounter with the criminal justice system forced his mother to make a difficult choice: lose her housing or ask her son to leave home. Jack's mother lives in housing that does not allow tenants to have criminal backgrounds. The landlord expressed to Jack's mother that he could not have sheriffs regularly visiting his building. Having to care for Jack's siblings, his mother was left with no other option but to ask Jack to leave home. This led to

Jack's housing instability, and he is now staying between the home of his uncle and that of his grandfather:

> I couldn't stay with my mom because the landlord wouldn't let me stay because I was on house arrest. The sheriffs come regularly to check on me and the landlord felt it would make his property look bad. So I couldn't stay with my mom, and there was no home phone to connect my ankle bracelet to.

Jack's experience reflects the larger experiences numerous poor families are forced into. Many affordable housing units have rules and regulations that prohibit tenants from renting if they have any type of conviction or felony on their record. These rules apply not only to the leaseholder, but also to any person residing in the home, regardless of their age or ability to care for themselves. These rules and regulations speak to the ways in which many folks of color who interface with the criminal justice system are discriminated against and excluded from access to federally assisted public housing (Alexander, 2010).

Prior to being allowed to stay with other family members, Jack lived on the street and in shelters for approximately two months. Although Jack is grateful for the generosity of his uncle and grandfather, he states:

> It feels like I'm in that type of situation [living on the street] right now. I have a "home" but as far as support, I feel alone, like no one's supporting me. You don't have to be on the street to be homeless.

Jack lacks the stable, consistent support of his biological parent. His experience also speaks to traditional definitions of homelessness, as they often do not differentiate between the varying degrees of homelessness that youth experience. Homelessness, as reported by Jack, is more than not having a place to stay every night; his experience encompasses the social–emotional aspects of instability. Some researchers suggest the term *housing distress*, defined as "the lack of a stable physical structure in which the adolescent feels he or she emotionally belongs" (Vissing & Diament, 1997, p. 34). This broader, more nuanced definition better captures the experiences of the youth in this study. It is important to recognize not only the physical but also the emotional factors that unstably housed youth experience, in an effort to capture a broad understanding of the many facets comprising the experiences of unaccompanied youth.

Jack's housing situation has led to inconsistent attendance and tardiness. Recognizing his need for support, Jack states:

My teachers help, I talk to them about my situation. I asked three of my teachers to write a recommendation for me so I can get off house arrest.

Some of Jack's teacher's are understanding of his predicament and serve as sources of support and guidance. These efforts have helped Jack to refocus and keep on track with his classes:

Thanks to those three teachers, I didn't fail my classes.

The support Jack received from these teachers in class allowed him to create a relationship, one in which he felt comfortable sharing his personal situation. As a result, Jack began receiving McKinney–Vento services:

Mr. Riley [homeless liaison] told me about the program to get a bus fare card, I don't have to pay for my school ID, I got a riding permit, and I didn't have to pay my school fees.

Jack's knowledge of the homeless education program at Diversey High is an indicator of effective minimal policy implementation. However, when presented with the Rights of Homeless Students Form (see Appendix B), Jack replied he had never been provided with the form. Jack's experience is indicative of the contradictory access and limitation of McKinney–Vento implementation occurring in schools.

Larger social–political perceptions of young Black males also influence Jack's experiences in the community and society at large:

I get treated differently just walking down the street, I get harassed by police. Even when I'm not doing anything wrong, the police just "jack" me.

Jack's run-ins with police, coupled with his previous arrests, has sparked his interest in and knowledge of the law, in particular his awareness of his legal rights, which has gotten him "noticed" by law enforcement. When the police have stopped him in the past, he questioned the cause of their detaining him. Since this incident, the police refer to him as "probable cause" due to his knowledge of his rights and often harass him based on this. Rather than being respected for his knowledge of his rights as a citizen, he instead is seen as a problem by authorities. Placing a racial lens on Jack's experience allows for the understanding that his racial identity in the larger social context is often associated with crime and delinquency. Jack's decision to become involved in illegal activity came out of his need to care for his basic needs. In poor communities of color, many young Black males see selling drugs as their only option. For Jack, this seemed to be the case:

> I started needing things like school supplies, bus money, winter clothing, and my mom wasn't able to get them for me, so I started selling drugs with my older brother.

Jack recognizes that his needs do not justify his actions; however, he also realizes that there is a real market out there for drugs. He points out the fact that he himself does not use drugs, and also that he does not have a line of family members that have been successful with legal means of making money. Jack is trying hard to stay out of trouble and is currently working to obtain summer employment recommended by a teacher. Recognizing the importance of school, Jack states:

> School will determine my future. It will decide how I make money.

Jack looks to his school to help support and guide his choices and decisions, with the short-term goal of being a successful student and the larger goal of obtaining legal employment that will serve to provide for his basic needs.

MICHAEL

"Come here, boy!" the voice startles me as I walk through the metal detectors of Grand High. The security guard continues, "Take your hat off; I'm not playing with you!" Students continue to enter the building 30 minutes after first period has started. As they enter, the security guard exclaims, "You need to be on time!" The student being reprimanded for his tardiness and rule infraction (wearing a hat) is Michael, a 15-year-old African American male in the 10th grade. As he removes his hat, a flattened afro emerges. He attempts to round it out, running his fingers through and around his hair. Head down, he slowly walks down the hallway to class.

Michael lives with his 19-year-old sister, her boyfriend, their daughter, and his mom's 37-year-old female friend. He also has a younger sister who attends a CPS elementary school and resides with their grandmother. His older sister is also enrolled in a CPS high school near their grandmother's home. Currently, Michael is under the care of his older sister due to his mother's drug involvement and subsequent incarceration, and he expresses difficulty in having to listen to her directions. Michael met the criteria for homelessness when his mother was incarcerated for illegal drug sales. Michael's mother tried to provide for her family, albeit illegally, which has resulted in her children not having a stable parent at home. Michael has considered selling drugs himself, as he has limited options for income, particularly with his mother currently absent from the home. Michael shares that his mother's friend does help out by caring for his niece while he and his older sister are at school. He misses his mother, and the fact that he cannot see her or ask her for help when he wants to. Michael shares that his mother's friend has lived with their family prior to his mother's incarceration and has always contributed to the household income. This dynamic may be an indicator of his family's financial status, prior to his mother's incarceration. Currently, his older sister and her boyfriend work to help support Michael and maintain their household. At home Michael must prepare himself for school and "stay on top of" his schoolwork with no parent or adult support.

The absence of Michael's mother has had a negative impact on his attendance. Michael shares that often he sleeps late, causing him to be consistently tardy. In a 2-week period, he usually misses about 2–3 days of school. He does not bring a note to explain his absence, nor does he ask to make up his work. He is aware that he can do well in school by completing all his school- and homework; however, he is not motivated or compelled to do so. According to Michael, his grades are "not too good" because of his tardiness. He explains that he never makes it to his first-period class, and some days he doesn't arrive at school until fourth period. In addition, his commute to school is an hour long. According to Michael, if his mom were home, he wouldn't be doing this. She would tell him to get out of the house and go to school. Michael smiles as he reflects on his mother's antics to get him up so he would arrive to school on time:

> When I won't wake up sometimes she would go outside, 'cause I have a window right next to my bed and she would knock on the window and make a lot of noise until I got up out the bed.

Although Michael recognizes his sister's efforts to serve in the capacity of "parent," due to their closeness in age it is difficult to take his sister seriously and adhere to her rules and advice. Despite Michael's tardiness, he continues to make an effort to attend school, even though he knows school staff will reprimand him for his extreme tardiness and many missed school days. Michael has not disclosed to his teachers his homeless situation, stating:

> If they were to know [I was homeless] they wouldn't treat me differently. I don't tell them because I don't think it would make a difference in how they were to me.

Michael's reluctance to share this information with his teachers may indicate his understanding of his teachers' disposition to provide support and counsel. It is apparent that Michael does not believe it will serve in his best interest to divulge this information. His sentiment may suggest a genuine feeling, or he may be trying to keep this information under wraps due to the stigma and stereotypes associated with homelessness. Michael shares that he went to the homeless liaison at his school at the urging of his older sister. Her knowledge of the homeless education program at her school allowed her to advise Michael on seeking out the homeless liaison at Grand High. The consistency of homeless liaisons within Michael's and his sister's schools is an example of an aspect of McKinney–Vento that is implemented. However, it also speaks to its shortcomings. If Michael's sister did not advise him, he would not have known of services provided through McKinney–Vento. This situation reflects a lack of McKinney–Vento implementation and accountability. Schools are required to identify and ensure students are aware of their rights under McKinney–Vento (NCLB/McKinney–Vento, 2002).

Michael also participates in an after-school program that offers students hands-on career experience and job training by allowing them to take part in arts, sports, technology, communications, and science programs. This program is run by a local nonprofit that provides services to teens in underserved communities and is in approximately 50 CPS high schools. Michael participates in the art program, describing to me a project in which he was able to design a shirt. The program takes place at Grand High from 4–7 p.m. 3 days a week, and Michael will be paid a small stipend for his participation; however, his ability to remain in the program may be jeopardized due to his absences from school. In addition, Michael is involved in his school's audiovisual program, which recently began running "Grand News." This 2-minute program covers topics important to students such as social events and extracurricular activities and is aired once a week on classroom televisions during Grand High's scheduled homeroom period. The program is produced by, written by, and stars Grand High students.

Grand High offers Michael many opportunities to participate in activities and become connected to school. During our conversation Michael also outlined areas in which Grand could improve and demonstrated his awareness of the dumbed-down curriculum and low expectations at his school:

> They need to update the books. All the other schools, the stuff they be learning sophomore year is things we learn as seniors. My friends tell me what they do at their school. Their classes are more challenging.

Although Michael currently faces challenges with attendance, he continues to make efforts to engage in his educational process, recognizing improvements that would motivate him to do better.

In terms of McKinney–Vento services, Michael receives fare cards to travel to and from school, but he is unable to identify other services he has received since seeking out the assistance of the homeless liaison, Ms. Gray. When I shared the Rights of Homeless Students Form with Michael, he stated:

> I've been receiving free breakfast and lunch since I was in grade [elementary] school, so that wasn't nothing new. But I've never gotten help with getting my uniform or any of the other stuff it says here. I borrow paper from my friends. It would have been helpful so I wouldn't have to pay for activities or pay for bus permits, and my fare cards don't always have the right amount on them.

Michael's commentary speaks to a very partial implementation of McKinney–Vento at Grand High. His family's experience with long-term poverty has provided him with access to services possibly covered under the provisions of Title I legislation. Outside of transportation services (receiving fare cards), Michael's other rights under McKinney–Vento are not being fulfilled.

The story of how Michael became homeless connects to his family's class standing, and this experience overlaps with his racial status in society as well. Further, Michael's experience with poverty mirrors the larger social contexts in which too many of our African American youth live. African Americans are disproportionately represented among single parent households, households having a parent that lives outside of the household due to incarceration, and households comprising people living in poverty. These realities are reflective of the inequitable treatment, system, and laws that marginalize and penalize Blacks at higher rates than their White peers (Alexander, 2010; Bell, 1973; Da Costa Nunez et al., 2012).

Despite the challenges he faces, Michael continues to attend school, working to remain engaged and connected to a consistent, stable space.

LEON

As I enter the office, Ms. Gray is on the phone: "They will not let him in the house, he's been living in an abandoned building. The other night someone tried to 'torch' the building while he was in it." Another counselor enters the office, "He showed up to school 'dirty.' The security guard is getting him clean clothes so he can shower." Ms. Gray hangs up the phone. "That was the Department of Child and Family Services. We need to get this student in somewhere." Ms. Gray, turns to me, stating, "He'll be a good student for you to speak with."

James, one of Grand High's security guards, takes me to meet with Leon, a 17-year-old African American male in his sophomore year. Leon's demeanor is mostly quiet, and he primarily looked down throughout our formal interview and informal interactions at Grand High. Leon does not have a consistent place he sleeps nightly, relying on the generosity of friends and family to take him in for the night. Occasionally, Leon is able to stay at his mother's or grandmother's house. Of all the youth interviewed, Leon's homeless situation is the most "typical" in terms of traditional notions of homelessness, which include staying in abandoned buildings and parks, riding the train, and doing whatever it takes in order find a place to sleep for the night.

Leon shares the family dynamics that contributed to his homeless condition:

Well, I've stayed in this situation since 8th grade, and I was starting off in grammar school after my great-grandmother had home schooled us. Once I got out of home school, I went to grammar school. I thought I couldn't make it there, and then after I went through all this stuff that my mother had put me through, that not trusting me, not loving me—when my daddy had died. Before he died, she was loving me and treating me nice, but since he died, I been living in abandoned buildings, trains, sneaking in people's backyards, and just sleeping in parks, and been scared sometimes, and when I got kicked out back and forth just because I took some pants from my brother and stuff . . . I try to go home and everything, she'll close her door, say you can't come here. She's acted, she's been changing and ever since that, he [dad] had died.

The rejection of Leon by his mother means he receives neither monetary nor emotional support from her. The instability Leon experiences influences his capacity to complete his schoolwork. Additionally, Leon feels that his mother's lack of belief in his ability to succeed has negatively impacted his educational experience,

> And really I didn't like it because going to school was really painful, because at school I gotta hide my pain inside from other teachers, and when I want to do something I can't do it because my mom had always told me that I couldn't make it and I feel that I couldn't.

Most of the school administration and staff are aware of Leon's situation, as he often arrives at school hungry, appearing disheveled, and unclean. Leon has an Individualized Education Program (IEP) and takes classes that focus on occupational preparation, rather than college preparation. Due to school officials' concerns about Leon's home situation, the Department of Child and Family Services was notified, creating an investigation of his mother and her care of him and his siblings. Leon also reports that he has run away from home "off and on" since 8th grade. Due to his mother's past boyfriends, he feels that his mother places more importance on the men in her life than she does on Leon:

> I always used to tell her, it's always about him, it's never about us, we are your kids.

At times, Leon has run away from home; at other times, his mother has been the one to initiate his departure from home. Furthermore, according to many of the school personnel who discussed Leon's situation, they suspect that Leon's mother has addiction issues. Leon also expressed this concern:

> One day I saw my mother's boyfriend the same day and he had gave me some change and everything, and I had told him, where's my mother, she still not home? So the pastor, he was driving me somewhere, and I saw my mother picking up something, a package from a man, then I cried, and I thought I knew what the package was, and the pastor had held my hand and said just pray for your mother. Then later, I heard she was in the hospital, and I wanted to come home, and then I thought she was hurt. I broke down crying in front of a lot of people, and the people who saw me crying just

started praying for me, and I said my mother's in the hospital for doing drugs, and I thought she was about to die or something.

Leon's concern for his mother's well being also has an impact on his mental health, as he repeatedly expressed worry over their relationship as well as her ability to care for herself and his siblings. These dynamics have an influence on his ability to engage in school.

Leon understands what a family should be and the depth of his loss in not having one, stating:

> Well, a family sometimes is supposed to be like, friends or people that come together as one and helps one another, but for me, its like I don't have a family.

Leon's description of family speaks to his feelings toward his personal situation in which he is not supported or included in family life.

In response, Leon has created relationships with many adults at Grand High. He regularly confides in these adults and seeks out their assistance. Specifically, he has befriended many of the security and lunchroom staff. According to Leon,

> The school, they been helping me with clothes, shoes, allowing me take showers, helping me with money, food, everyday that I'm at school.
> When I come in and they know that my clothes dirty, they'll sometimes give me new shirts, new jeans, new coats, hats, and sometimes they know that I'm hungry, they give me some food, when they not supposed to sometimes.

When asked who it is who actually helps him, he answered:

> The security guards. They give me clothes, the same people, Johnson, Barnes, Holloway [security staff], they give me clothes, let me take showers, and give me stuff that I really need.

Here we see school staff providing services that should be addressed through direct service or service referral through McKinney–Vento. Without the charitable contributions of staff, Leon would not be provided with support of his educational services that directly relate to his student role, such as having a clean uniform for school.

Leon was determined to maintain his attendance. He would come to school daily, whether or not he had a place to sleep the night before, was able to clean up, or secure a meal. Some days he did not have clean clothes, or the appropriate clothes (school uniform) for school. He was teased and chastised by students and teachers alike but still found the motivation to engage in school daily. Leon's experience with school personnel other than the security staff led to his eventual mistrust of these adults. Due to the fact that Leon did not have a consistent place to stay, his appearance made it apparent that he was having bouts with homelessness. For this reason, initially the staff seemed to have a sincere desire to help Leon. However, as he continued to exhibit behavioral problems in school (getting into fights, stealing), the staff had less empathy for his situation. As a result, staff would sometimes speak openly about his situation. In addition, some staff "warned" me not to trust Leon, making comments such as "watch your purse," while others commented on his lack of hygiene: "Have you seen him today, his clothes are all dirty and he stinks!" Leon's presence became problematic for school administrators, to the point where he was suspended from school for "being dirty," when in fact they were denying him needed access, support, and referrals as required and outlined under McKinney–Vento. Even still, Leon made the effort to attend his classes.

As the year progresses, the instability impacting his self-care and behavior begins to have negative consequences. According to Leon, the school stopped allowing him to shower after they talked to his mother:

[The principal feels] it's my fault, it's nothing that deals with school, it's a mother and son thing and we have to deal with it because that's messing up my school time.

In one instance, Leon had come to school and didn't have a chance to clean up and the principal sent him home. Leon explained:

Well, I really wasn't going to come to school after my mother, we had this little fight and it was like we was in the alley fighting, and then she said get out of her face. So I said, well this is not going to mess up my education. I came to school and I thought school was just for to get an education and graduate, and just because I didn't clean up or nothing, 'cause I couldn't and no police officer would help, they look at me like I'm special ed., but really I'm not, and they said, well go home and do that (clean up), they suspended me for something I couldn't do, which was my mother's fault. I was suspended because I didn't clean up.

It appears that the initial kindness and patience many of the school staff displayed wanes as the school year progresses. School staff Leon initially identified as sources of support, after time show little tolerance for his unclean clothing and the other issues he brings to school. Here McKinney–Vento is poorly implemented, and the lack of implementation undermined both Leon's emotional support and education. With either unawareness or indifference to the provisions of the law, and in direct violation of it, Grand High did not ensure that students experiencing homelessness received necessary services. It is left to individuals to decide whether or not they will help these students. Further, because Leon is not aware of his rights to services and referrals under McKinney–Vento, he is unable to hold school officials accountable for their actions, or lack thereof. For Leon, this not only means an end to resources and support, but it also results in a disruption to his schooling. This also affects Leon's interactions with school staff:

> They (teachers and students at Grand High) talk about me when I come through the school door.
> They always talk about, well we gotta deal with Leon again, and here we go again, they think negative instead of positive things.
> It makes me feel bad.

Leon's experiences not only have an impact on his physical ability to attend school, they also influence his mood and overall emotional well-being. Leon's descriptions of his interactions with staff extend to his larger perceptions and understandings of African Americans more generally. As Leon reflects on his situation, he observes:

> Because Blacks really, I gotta be careful how I say, Blacks really, to me they are uncareable people.
> Because, I don't know how to put it. To me because Black people, it's like everybody's making it out like, like we're not gonna make it because of the kids. Blacks OK, what's going on, on like the news and everything, Black people have done most crimes or sometimes, Black people, they just hate each other for no reason.

Asked if he feels this way due to personal experience, Leon shares:

> What I see on TV and sometimes out in the world, parents are always beating up, kicking their kids out, instead of talking about it, that's what I see, sometimes as I'm out here.

While Leon's own family experience and his experience of his community might produce these judgments, media also plays a role in presenting the African American persona as a negative one. This exposure contributes to popular perceptions and stereotypes associated with African Americans. These images, coupled with Leon's negative experiences with his mother and insensitive treatment by teachers, contribute to Leon's negative perception. He goes on to state:

> Maybe the kid did something that they, that their parents did when they was younger. Instead of saying well, well parents do tell them that they did it, when they was younger, the thing is that us kids, what kids supposed to be to their parent, someone that they should care about and be treated like a young adult, because that's what they're going to grow up to be and if parents treat them like that, why grow up to be nothing, when you could grow up to be something?

He goes on to state:

> Well Blacks to me, is really too much and really for a Black person because, to me a child is a person that really should be with their parents and not without their parents, but I could see that sometimes that it's not really the parent or the child's fault, it's really like, they're homeless, because the parents and the child are either kicked out the house because they haven't been paying any rent or because the parent didn't want their child there and just because the parent didn't want their child there, it's not a reason to for her to kick the person out on the street, in the cold.

In addition to Leon's personal experience of becoming homeless, he also recognizes the structural forces that render African Americans homeless. One's inability to maintain their housing is usually due to limited access to affordable housing, loss of employment, or underemployment. The massive gentrification occurring in Chicago has placed a disproportionate amount of Blacks and Latinas/os in these predicaments.

Despite many limitations, Leon maintains his school attendance, focusing his efforts on remaining engaged in school:

> Well, homeless or not, an education is something that's really important, because if you're at home and you don't have that paper

that says I graduated from high school, you won't get nowhere in life. Well if you're homeless, and that'll really help you to get the jobs that would accept you for the education that you have done.

Leon's understanding of the importance of school to his future serves as a motivator guiding his decision to remain in school.

In a struggle to acquire basic shelter outside of school, Leon regularly sleeps in abandoned buildings. Due to this activity, Leon was arrested for trespassing and missed almost a full week of school. The homeless liaison, Ms. Gray, received a call from Leon's grandmother informing her of this situation. Despite his grandmother's concern, due to financial constraints, she was not able to bail Leon out of jail. Leon also provided me with his experience of the situation:

Well, since I got me and this friend had got mad that my mother didn't let me in after school. So he had said since the building is closed, I'm gonna go break in this building and you just sit here and look; so I just stayed there trying to be the watch out because I was too cold, and when he broke in, the police had finally saw us, and they knew I didn't do it, they found the guy who did it, but he threw both of us in jail and I was just in jail scared.

Once released, Leon returned to school. Despite the barriers Leon faces, his desire to maintain some sense of consistency in his life pushes him to attend school, working to maintain his connections to school staff. Leon's persistence is awarded through his participation in the school's "half-gown" honor ceremony. Grand High has implemented a program that aims to motivate students who have completed their sophomore year, serving as a preview to their final senior graduation. The ceremony resembles graduation; students are provided with the honor of walking across the stage in a cap and gown, their parents/guardians and up to three guests are invited to attend. Grand High was able to acquire a very special guest to their ceremony, a high-ranking administrator within CPS's central office. This administrator praised the students for completing their first two years of high school, encouraging them to continue on so he may attend their senior graduation. Furthermore, he pledges to provide summer internships to all students with perfect attendance and a minimum of a "B" average. A small reception is held in a meeting room in the school where snacks and beverages are provided for students and their families.

CHAPTER 3

Awareness, Understanding, and Accountability

Homeless is a situation, It's not who you are.

—*The Homestretch*, 2014

There are several adults in the school context that work to cultivate and support opportunities and facilitate access for students to achieve both academically and personally. The purpose of this chapter is to focus on the role adults can play in the lives of youth experiencing housing instability. The McKinney–Vento Act requires that districts and schools designate an adult in the school building that serves as a homeless liaison (NCLB, 2002). However, the language is vague, allowing for multiple interpretations of the specific roles and responsibilities of homeless liaisons. As I will show in this chapter, liaisons take on several roles in working to ensure the rights of students are preserved. However, there are several structural factors inherent in the school system that limit their ability to do so.

Liaisons are not the only individuals charged with ensuring rights of homeless students in Chicago. The Chicago Public School system employs an administrator that oversees proper implementation of McKinney–Vento for the entire school district. Further, due to previous litigation between CPS and students/families experiencing homelessness (Dohrn, 1991; Salazar v. Edwards, 2004), there is also a Chicago-based organization that works on behalf of families and students across the state to hold Illinois school districts, including CPS, accountable for upholding students' rights as outlined in the law. The voices of these various adults will be featured in the discussions below.

DIVERSEY HIGH

Diversey High has open enrollment, allowing all students living within its attendance area to be eligible for admittance. By CPS standards, the school has "average" enrollment. In regards to academics, the average ACT score at Diversey High is well below the state standard. Within Diversey High there are two small schools—a remedial school and a military school—in addition to the general high school. My observations of Diversey High took place largely in the general high school. However, because one of the smaller schools, the remedial school, had its own homeless liaison, I spent time there as well.

Staff, Climate, and Culture

In addition to formal interviews with the homeless liaisons at Diversey High, there were opportunities for informal exchanges with several counselors, social workers, teachers, teacher aides, security personnel, and other paraprofessionals working within the school. When these various school staff came to speak with Mr. Riley or Ms. Franklin in their respective offices, they would often share their thoughts, frustrations, and insights regarding students in general and homeless students in particular. During one of these encounters, a social worker shared:

> I find myself wanting to wash my hands to avoid germs: they [homeless people] are not very clean, [they] don't keep up with their hygiene.

He went on to say:

> Many of these [homeless] kids have unrealistic goals of college. They don't have the grades or test scores to be in college. I don't think college is for everyone. I tell them what they need is a skill set, something they can do to help them make money. If they get a trade, make $20 an hour, that's pretty good; not everyone is college material. I think it's good for those who can do it, but it's not for everyone.

Although this social worker believed he was helping, it is apparent by the language and attitude he displayed during our interaction that he views homeless individuals in a particular way; his beliefs stem from a deficit approach (Nieto, 1996) by which he believes that the homeless students he comes across should focus more on skills (blue-collar employment) than higher education (white-collar employment). His comments reflect the lowered expectations this particular adult has of youth experiencing homelessness.

During observations at Diversey High, racialization processes would play themselves out through day-to-day interactions. Some examples of this include student writing on bathroom stalls that read: "This is a hate crime, Mexicans go back to your country!" In another instance, I was asked to retrieve students from their classrooms, as their parents were arriving to collect them from school for the Thanksgiving holiday. As I went back and forth in the hallways, I passed an older White male teacher a few times. During one of our encounters, I stated there were a lot of early dismissals today, to which he responded, "They probably all need to leave early to drive to Mexico" (fieldnotes, November 21, 2007). Negative or stereotypical comments were not only made by Whites in reference to Latinas/os or Blacks; staff of the same race also held some of these beliefs. A Latina staff member, during an impromptu discussion regarding youth and their spending habits commented, "Blacks and some Hispanics are really bad; they spend $300 on a phone bill but don't have money for a car" (fieldnotes, February 20, 2008). Another teacher "jokingly" commented about going to an off-site meeting on the south side of Chicago, asking his colleague, "Did you see me getting mugged?" He went on to explain how he walked "very quickly" to the building from the train station, because had he been aware of the neighborhood in which the meeting was held, he would have driven (fieldnotes, November 28, 2007). Although these comments were said in jest, the implication is that if you are on the south side of the city (which is predominantly Black), the perception is that you are more likely to be victimized (getting mugged), and one needs to be extra cautious about one's surroundings because of the people comprising the community population (Black folks).

Other staff members interpret these dynamics differently. When I spoke with a Latina teacher, she commented, "Many of the kids are put down at home. They're told they're dumb and won't amount to anything." Understanding this, she feels it is her responsibility to provide them with unconditional support and encouragement: "Even if they're late, I'll say 'good to see you, glad you came to school today'" (fieldnotes, November 28, 2007). This teacher's response to the students' needs reflects her understanding of the students' experiences, allowing her to provide opportunities for the youth to engage positively in school. These actions by staff are especially important for youth of color experiencing homelessness due to their social status within school systems. Consistent, caring support from an adult can significantly shape a student's experience in school (Graves & Howes, 2011).

Additionally, some teachers recognized the racial categorization that functions within schools and sought to address these issues head-on with students. At Diversey High, a White male social studies teacher generated an after-school group entitled Race Matters. This group ran for 5 weeks (meeting one time per week) and consisted of discussions regarding issues of racism and other "isms" such as sexism. Race Matters was a small group of about six students, and its racial makeup included two African American female students and one African American male student, two Latinas, and one Indian male student. The teacher leading this group shared his interest in providing a place for students to discuss issues of race, particularly in schools. He stated, "Even if people think to ignore race, we should be talking about that, whatever *it* is" (fieldnotes, February 26, 2008). The students created and disseminated a survey that addressed issues of race in their school and planned to share the results with the school as a whole. As the students tallied the survey responses, they shared information on the two presidential candidates (Barack Obama and Hillary Clinton), delving into issues of race and gender. One student shared with the group a program he had viewed on C-SPAN with Cornel West and a policy person from Capitol Hill addressing the inequities faced by African Americans in the United States. The students, teacher, and I engaged in a brief discussion about the significance of race and gender in the election and its future implications should either candidate become president (fieldnotes, February 26, 2008). This group was somewhat of an anomaly in the school, as most other teachers and staff did not engage in critical discussions of race, gender, or class.

Racial dimensions of the school environment are highlighted here to illuminate the underpinnings of race, its pervasiveness in the social and systemic structure of schools, and its relationship with poverty and educational policy for homeless students. Addressing these dynamics aids in the larger understanding of the role race plays in the structure and function of schools. It also illuminates the many ways in which meaningful and productive conversations regarding race are omitted from these spaces.

Mr. Riley

On the way into the curriculum office there were many signs posted meant to encourage students' reading, such as "Achieve!" and "Knowledge Is Power!" The school's bell schedule was posted along the back wall of the office. This large space contained giant windows adjacent to the school's main entrance. Five computers lined the back wall along with several stacks of curriculum documents and other school forms. A purple and yellow poster indicating that Mr. Riley was the homeless liaison of Diversey High was also posted, an indicator of McKinney–Vento compliance. The sign provided students who might be experiencing homelessness with his contact information, a definition and criteria of *homelessness*, along with a phone number to the homeless education program administrative offices of CPS. Mr. Riley shared that, due to the many budget cuts within CPS, his staff had been significantly cut over the last couple of years from a five-person team down to two people, he and his assistant, Ms. Lopez. Mr. Riley provided an overview of his responsibilities as homeless liaison, consisting mainly of paperwork that needs to be completed for students to be enrolled in the homeless education program. Once enrolled, students receive free breakfast and lunch, fee waivers, and fare cards for transportation (for those who had to travel more than one mile to attend school). He also shared that just the other day a school counselor turned a homeless student away. His role as homeless liaison is to inform and educate all school staff of the requirements of McKinney–Vento. He needed to go speak with the entire counseling staff about not turning students away. Instead, they should refer them to Mr. Riley for assistance (fieldnotes, October 10, 2007). In passing, Mr. Riley shared that the past assistant principal did not like homeless students and would regularly turn them away, refusing their enrollment—a direct violation of McKinney–Vento.

Mr. Riley continued to share his roles and responsibilities as homeless liaison, furnishing the many forms that needed to be completed in order for students experiencing homelessness to obtain support. These documents included an emergency form, a school waiver form, and an enrollment form. Once filled out, the forms are to then be faxed to CPS's Central Office for approval. Once Central Office approves students for the homeless education program, the school is provided with bus fare cards for all eligible students. Providing transportation for students is a requirement under McKinney–Vento. This removes the barrier of transportation, guaranteeing students experiencing homelessness transportation to and from school daily. Students are to receive two fare cards per day (one to get to school, and one to get "home" at the end of the school day). In addition, Mr. Riley is required to complete electronic forms to ensure students are identified as homeless within the CPS system. Finally, students and families experiencing homelessness are to receive a Notice of Dispute Resolution Form, and a Rights of Homeless Students Form (see Appendix B).

In early October there were 53 students identified and eligible for services under McKinney–Vento at Diversey High (fieldnotes, October 10, 2007). As the year progressed, some students did not remain in the school, resulting in 44 students identified as homeless. As part of Mr. Riley's daily routine, a few minutes prior to the end of the day, he pulls out a small locked box that contains fare cards and a self-made "McKinney–Vento Transportation List, " in preparation for disseminating fare cards to students. The bell rang, indicating the end of the classes for the day. Students began to file into the office, lining up at the counter to receive their fare cards. In order to receive the cards, students must sign their name on the transportation list as well as show their school ID upon request. This allows Mr. Riley to track use of fare cards for the school. Mr. Riley states that he is familiar with most of the faces, though sometimes he may ask if he isn't sure. Referring to the process and procedure of disbursing fare cards to students, he also shares that the method in place is "not how I'm supposed to do it, but it works this way" (fieldnotes, October 10, 2008). Due to issues of confidentiality, students should be provided these services without knowledge of others. By default, this process exposes students to each other, as each is aware they are in line for fare cards due to their status as homeless. Confidentiality is a component of McKinney–Vento that is disregarded by the process implemented in both Diversey and Grand as well as other schools (De Mare & Kelly, 2014).

As students file into and out of the office, Mr. Riley provides commentary: "He's 16, but still a freshman," "Those two girls are from Malawi and they don't speak English well." After about 20 minutes, the majority of students listed on the McKinney–Vento transportation form had signed the list and left the school building for the day. Students are required to sign this form once a day, to document who receives fare cards under McKinney–Vento.

As the hustle and bustle of student traffic dissipates, Mr. Riley provides further description of his responsibilities as homeless liaison. He was to provide an inservice training to the school staff within the first two months of the school year in order to inform all school personnel of the criteria of homeless student service eligibility and the identification processes. In essence, if a teacher or other staff member believes a student is homeless, they are to contact the homeless liaison. Once the liaison is informed, he is to meet with the student and determine their homelessness status. Mr. Riley's thorough and comprehensive understanding of the forms and other procedural requirements of his role as homeless liaison was impressive. His sincerity and effort to provide homeless students with services was extremely refreshing.

Mr. Riley has been in the position of homeless liaison for over 10 years. Prior to being assigned the homeless liaison responsibilities, Mr. Riley had no prior experience working with homeless families or students. The three homeless liaisons who participated in this project all described similar circumstances. Their principals assigned them this duty, sometimes despite their reluctance due to their inexperience with individuals experiencing homelessness. Further, they explained that they had not been provided additional time, funding, or resources to fulfill their homeless liaison responsibilities as well as those of their primary positions as teachers or administrators. McKinney–Vento policy clearly outlines the requirement that all schools/districts have a homeless liaison. However, the policy does not specify criteria for designating these individuals, nor a monetary incentive or compensation for the time and effort required to fulfill these responsibilities.

Discussing the needs and difficulties of students experiencing homelessness, Mr. Riley states:

> They each come in with their own set of background issues. Some of the students are actually in shelters, some of the students are doubled-up, some of the students are runaways, some of the students are throwaways, so every student comes in with very different issues. And some of our students live in the neighborhood, and others live on the south, far south, and far west sides [of Chicago], so that all affects how they are here at school, affects their grades and their progress.

Mr. Riley's assessment of the many young people he has encountered over the years as homeless liaison reflects the diversity of the issues and obstacles youth are up against. These range from traveling far distances to experiencing family conflict. He also addresses the differences he sees among unaccompanied youth as compared to their accompanied counterparts (refer to Chapter 1 for definitions):

> Because of the instability for those students, their attendance is much poorer than other students. And then they don't have a fixed place to go at night, so there's really no way that a study environment can be provided, so it's very difficult for them to do homework assignments, do research projects or whatever because they just don't have that kind of stability. And they don't have the resources that a shelter would provide or that a parent would provide, living with another

relative, and then just because the attendance is so much poorer, there's no continuity from day to day in their education. So it's more likely that they are going to experience failure in their classes and not develop the kinds of social relationships that the other students develop because of the situation they're in.

This commentary reflects the additional barriers unaccompanied youth face due to their lack of stability and support from a consistent adult. Issues of instability impact the students' ability to complete work and be engaged in class. These factors serve as barriers to school engagement and success.

It is of note that younger unaccompanied homeless students (aged 15 and under) often had links to social service agencies prior to their contact with the homeless liaison. Mr. Riley often spends more time speaking with students who are 15 years old and younger. In his experience, youth of this age who are unaccompanied usually are in contact with a social service agency. It is usually the social service agency that will bring the adolescent to school to be enrolled. So while these students are not in the direct care of an adult, they often have access to an adult figure through the social service agency. These agencies assist youth with housing, transportation, clothing, and food. These services are an example of aspects of the larger homeless policy that is working well for students.

However, for older youth, it is the homeless liaison who connects them to services or agencies for basic needs as well as support. Mr. Riley explains:

OK, what we generally do is, I work with the counselors and the school social worker to make sure that we're providing as many services as we can for those students. I work with the social worker who has direct contact with a number of social service agencies throughout Chicago to make sure that a student can be plugged in with one of those, one or more of those social service agencies. That student can get the kind of counseling he or she needs, provisions for food and shelter that are needed, just to make sure that there's basic services.

This is especially important for unaccompanied youth that are not in the care of an adult. It also demonstrates the school's efforts to provide nonacademic services. These services are significant as they play a role in the students' overall well-being, which ultimately impacts their academic success.

Early in the school year Mr. Riley conducted a mandatory homeless education training to the entire school staff. As a result of this training, many teachers voiced concern for homeless students and suggested taking donations around the holidays in order to purchase gifts for homeless students (fieldnotes, November 2, 2007). Two teachers in particular led this effort through a club that focuses on peace, nonviolence, and unity. In the past this club has raised money for other charitable causes and viewed the predicament of homeless students as an opportunity to raise awareness and offer charitable contributions. The group was successful. Students and teachers were able to raise money for students experiencing homelessness at Diversey High. These funds were to be used to purchase items for the students or provide them with gift cards to spend the money as they chose.

Several times Mr. Riley addressed the ways in which other agencies and he himself offered charitable contributions. When asked about how he collects funds and materials to support students, he explained:

> It's an in-house type of thing; generally I've gone to a number of teachers and asked if they'd be willing to contribute, depending on who the student knows or who the student has as a teacher in class. Sometimes we're able to provide the things for them that they need, sometimes we aren't. The board does not provide funding for parents per se. They will provide what they call hardship transportation for students who are 6th grade or under. Once the students are in 7th grade the board says no, they're adult enough that they can come and go to school on their own. However, the school does provide adult fare cards for parents to come to the school for report card pickup days, both in November and April. What I've done, around here again, is, just out of my own pocket, is buy cards at Dominick's to provide some payment, so that they may have transportation. Outside of report card pickup, let's say if the parent comes into the building because their child was suspended or there was a disciplinary issue, parent conference, or whatever, and they happen to come to my office, then I will make sure that they don't leave my office without a full fare card to get back, but that's not something that the board provides, that's something that I provide.

Although McKinney–Vento funds do not cover all costs to assist with parents' participation in their child's educational lives, Mr. Riley recognizes the importance of parent engagement. Of his own volition, he provides this service to the students and families at Diversey High. Mr. Riley should be praised for his kindness. However, what about the schools that don't have a Mr. Riley? It is important to consider the funding that is allocated to McKinney–Vento. Research reveals that McKinney–Vento funding is inadequate (Wong et al., 2009); current federal funds are not sufficient in supporting the academic needs of students experiencing instability (CCH, 2014). In 2009, Illinois dedicated 3 million dollars to supplement the federal funds—funding that has not been renewed since (CCH, 2014). At the federal level, funding has remained flat, despite a 72% increase in homeless students since 2006–2007. According to the Chicago Coalition for the Homeless (CCH, 2014), "Illinois receives $5 million in federal funding to serve 859 school districts. Of those, only eight districts directly receive federal funding. The remaining funding goes to regional offices of education or lead liaisons that serve as many as 100 school districts, with limited ability to provide direct services to individual homeless students or families" (p. 2).

In regard to the many needs of homeless students, Mr. Riley shared these thoughts:

> In some cases it's simple requests such as not having school supplies, not having clothing. Some of them have to come to me and said that the only two meals that they get per day are the breakfast and lunch that we serve here. And so, some of them have asked me personally for my money just so they can get some sort of decent meal in the evenings. Certainly, the kids who are throwaways and runaways, it's much more prevalent with them, because they're out on the streets either begging for money or engaging in activities that we would frown upon to get the money to do that. Generally we try to help the seniors because of all the senior activities; we want the seniors to be able to participate in those types of activities. So teachers and myself will usually pay for the senior luncheon, we'll pay for the students to go to prom. I can only provide so many services, the social worker would then work with those young people to at least set up appointments at counseling agencies and that sort of thing. But again, based on their living situation, chances are they might go to the appointment, they might not.

As Mr. Riley's comments demonstrate, students' needs range from monetary to emotional support. While there are many efforts in place to support homeless students, these are often in the form of individual efforts. However, there is a lack of systemic structure in place to ensure that students receive needed services; this lack of structure is connected to insufficient funding that would allow liaisons the additional time, support, and training required to adequately meet the needs of students experiencing instability.

While McKinney–Vento requires schools to provide students with services, often schools are not provided with the human and monetary resources necessary to ensure that all students experiencing housing in-stability receive the services and support needed to fully engage in the educational process. McKinney–Vento mandates that every school have a designated liaison charged with providing assistance and services to homeless students. For many schools, this means that staff is provided with additional job responsibilities; however they are not compensated for their time or provided with more time to complete their primary job responsibilities. For example, Mr. Riley identified time constraints that limit him from fully engaging in his role as homeless liaison:

> Well, that's the way it has been here, I think partly because there are
> so many students. I have to make sure that all of the administrative
> things are taken care of. And I sometimes—since I don't have a
> counseling degree, it's better left in the hands of the counselors and
> social workers to provide those kinds of services. However, at other
> schools where other people serve as the homeless liaisons, they don't
> have such a large caseload as I have, and so then they're able to get
> more personally involved with the students, and they work with
> the parents as well, in providing those kinds of services. They may
> not have counseling degrees either, but because they just have far
> fewer demands on their time, they're able to provide those types of
> relationships and they get to know the parents much more intimately
> than I do.

He goes on to talk about his primary position as curriculum coordinator:

> I think that's just the nature of the role of curriculum coordinator;
> probably it's not the best pairing of the two, and in area Z which
> is all of the high schools west of A avenue, I think there's only one
> other high school where the curriculum coordinator is also the
> homeless liaison, usually it's a counselor. Sometimes it's a parent
> representative or volunteer, sometimes it's one of the clerks in the
> main office and I think that based on the number of students that
> we have here, probably someone else would do a far more thorough
> job of providing the kinds of services that these students really need.
> But staffing has been reduced so each person now is being asked to

do more with less. At this point I don't know who that principal might choose to be homeless liaison, if I was asked to be relieved of that duty. But I think it's very difficult at this point to have a curriculum coordinator also be the homeless liaison in light of the large caseload. If it were only 5 students it would be no problem. I could definitely provide those 5 students with many more services than I could provide to 44.

Time is an issue for Mr. Riley, as well as the poor fit between his primary position as curriculum coordinator and his "extra" responsibility of homeless liaison. This well-intentioned but piecemeal approach to filling the need for a homeless liaison also has implications for the policy description and implementation. While McKinney–Vento outlines that an individual serve as homeless liaison, it does not specify the qualifications or background needed. Unaccompanied homeless youth, especially, require several unique types of support. The adults charged with providing services should be qualified to implement best practices for these needs.

In addition to inquiring about McKinney–Vento implementation from Mr. Riley's perspective, I raised the issue of the overrepresentation of students of color comprising the homeless student population at Diversey High, as well as the larger school system. During the time of our interview, there were 43 homeless students identified. Of these, 39 were African American and 4 were Latina/o. When I inquired about these racial disparities, Mr. Riley responded:

The students that live in our attendance area tend to be of lower socioeconomic status. . . . Until recently the surrounding neighborhoods had large apartments and large homes that were subdivided into smaller apartments and rented . . . to people with lower socioeconomic status than the rest of the city. But I think because we are working with students who meet the federal poverty guidelines, I think 94% of the students at our school meet those guidelines. These are the people who are marginally on the edge, and their parents struggle to maintain a job; if the job disappears, if they lose that particular job, then they're finding that they can't afford to stay in their apartment. And very quickly they lose the apartment, and then either have to go into a shelter or have to double up with other people. So we're talking people that don't have a lot of means, don't have a lot of resources, and are probably one paycheck away from being homeless.

Mr. Riley's response on the surface appears to be void of language pertaining to race, focusing his commentary on issues seemingly related to class. This framing is similar to the way in which the larger society frames homelessness. However, from a critical race theory and structural racism approach, one must ask, who are these people of low socioeconomic status? Marginally on the edge? Meeting the federal poverty level guidelines? Unpacking Mr. Riley's homeless language is important to understanding the group of people he is describing. It may also be indicative of a lack of awareness or willingness to engage the disparate outcomes for youth of color generally, and specifically youth of color experiencing homelessness that he encounters daily. While Mr. Riley was reluctant to engage the issue of race as it relates to homeless students, it is understandable due to the tensions that often surround conversations centered on race. Due to the delicate nature of the topic, Mr. Riley (and other school teachers/staff) may find it uncomfortable and even politically incorrect to address race. However, since African American students are overrepresented among the homeless student population in the district, it is critical to begin to unpack the systems and processes that may be contributing to these racial and class disparities.

Mr. Riley's enthusiasm and energy waned as the school year progressed. Soon after the winter break until the end of the school year, Mr. Riley's attendance became very sporadic, which caused issues for students and families seeking out services that required the assistance of the homeless liaison. This also caused stress and tension for his assistant, Ms. Lopez, who was not equipped to carry out the many tasks of the curriculum office, nor those related to homeless students. Although it became apparent to teachers and staff that Mr. Riley was not fulfilling his responsibilities as curriculum coordinator or as homeless liaison, on the surface, nothing was said or done to address it. Ms. Lopez expressed her frustration regarding his absence, stating, "They [administration] know he's not here, what can I do?" (fieldnotes, April 30, 2008). In addition, Ms. Lopez shared that the money collected for homeless students at Diversey High had never been disbursed to the students, stating, "Who is going to get that money?" (fieldnotes, June 6, 2008). During Mr. Riley's absence it became apparent that a person's disposition regarding these responsibilities was crucial in students being provided with the needed services. Although the school clerk and principal were also trained in the roles and responsibilities required by McKinney–Vento, neither appeared to fill that role in his absence. By the end of the school year, Mr. Riley retired, expressing his frustration that the school had not yet identified his replacement as homeless liaison, and consequently he was not able to provide them with the appropriate training on his roles and responsibilities.

While it may seem easy to point the finger at Mr. Riley or others, their actions reflect larger systemic issues. Without systems in place to ensure accountability and enforcement of McKinney–Vento, we cannot guarantee that students and families experiencing homelessness obtain the access, support, and services they are entitled to. The dynamics occurring at Diversey High are a reflection of this school's lack of structural support for ensuring appropriate implementation of McKinney–Vento. Failure to construct this critical infrastructure resulted in several students and families who were experiencing homelessness not receiving services that could have facilitated the students' ability to more fully engage in their educational endeavors. Mr. Riley's retirement, and his physical and emotional withdrawal in advance of it, effectively magnified the crisis of homelessness already experienced by 44 students. This situation also speaks to larger policy issues that should be addressed, such as more specific language, criteria, funding, and external review and enforcement, to support proper implementation and increase accountability.

Ms. Franklin

As Diversey High was made up of three separate schools (all housed in one building), there were two homeless liaisons within Diversey High. Ms. Franklin served as a homeless liaison for one of the complementary schools. This school focused on students who were of high school age but did not have sufficient credits to be in the "traditional" school. Ms. Franklin was often found in her office occupied with paperwork or speaking with students and/or parents. Her office was the first door near the entrance to the main office, which also contained the school clerk and other offices. In addition to the basic furniture found in most school offices (desks, chairs, shelves, and so on) there were boxes of remedial curriculum materials scattered around the newly renovated office space shared by various school personnel (e.g., counselors, ancillary staff). This renovation was the result of a recent donation made to the school by various organizations and individuals. The majority of the student body, however, was learning below the 9th-grade level. Within this office is also a small room that serves as a counseling office for pregnant and parenting youth. These services are part of a program created to keep pregnant and parenting students enrolled in school.

Ms. Franklin expressed her interest in my research and voiced her concern that not enough research is completed at the high school level for students in general, and for homeless students in particular. She also shared her frustration with the paperwork that needed to be completed for homeless students, commenting that often the person overseeing homeless student correspondence for their particular area was disrespectful to her, ultimately having a negative affect on homeless students within the school. While this does not prevent students from receiving services, the processing and subsequent services are often delayed. Ms. Franklin noted that, due to the smaller school size, there were not as many homeless students—approximately five—and of those, possibly two would meet the criteria of unaccompanied.

Ms. Franklin has been a counselor for over 15 years. Additionally, she has personal experiences with homelessness; as an adult she was rendered homeless due to a domestic violence situation. Ms. Franklin expresses her awareness of the barriers students experiencing homelessness face and is empathetic to their needs. In regard to the general characteristics of homeless students, Ms. Franklin shared:

> They come in all shapes, sizes, and forms. I can't say that there's any one particular thing about homeless children that's all alike. I've had children that have lived in hotels, I've had those that have lived in shelters, many that have been doubled-up. People, kids that have pretty much lived by themselves, kids awaiting placement in DCFS—girls, boys. I had one child, about two years ago I think it was, who was homeless and had two children of her own. Well, she was pregnant at the time and then she delivered, and I remember trying to call shelters to see if they would take her in. But shelters don't take people in until they're 18, ya know, so she wasn't in the system. She had avoided being in the system and as a result she had been in the system, got out of the system some kind of way, I guess. She probably, I don't know how she got out of the system but she did. And at the time that I worked with [her] she was, like I said, pregnant with another baby, then she had the baby, and things didn't work out very well. I hear from her every now and then.

Her statement is reflective of the nuanced experiences unstably housed students find themselves in. Young people experiencing homelessness struggle to obtain stability and consistency in their lives. For some youth, this experience includes also serving in the role of parent. As we continued our discussion, she had this to say:

When a child lives with his or her parent, they have a parent there; even if they're doubled-up, it's not the same as when a child is in a shelter with a parent or without a parent; or if a child is totally unaccompanied, there's a big difference. I think that in the case of most of the homeless children, as I recollect, most of them were literally disorganized, and until they find a permanent residence, or someplace where they are consistently, there's so much family drama or drama based on where they're living that it just disrupts them in being able to function; they don't function well at all.

For students in the situation Ms. Franklin describes, their instability negatively impacts their educational experiences. Research demonstrates that emotional health influences and shapes student learning (Durlak, Weissburg, & Pachan, 2010). Stability is a key component needed for the overall development of all youth. For unaccompanied youth experiencing homelessness, their lack of stability outside of school limits the support they need to meaningfully engage in their student role.

Acknowledgement of the issues homeless youth encounter is the first step to addressing their needs. Student requests are many and require the work of several key players. Ms. Franklin offered:

I try to do what I can, and the other people around here try and do what they can for these kids. There are times when we feed 'em, we may have something around here and we'll get them something to eat, because we know that there is no parent at home fixing them a meal and that kind of thing so, we do that.

Students experiencing housing instability are in need of food, housing, clothing, and other necessary things; had they not been offered these services, goods, and support from caring individuals, it is probable their situation would have been much worse. "If some portion of voluntary resources are not directed at solving the root causes of social problems, we exhaust our ability to create the social structures that operate for the greater good and create a permanent underclass" (Marullo & Edwards, 2000, p. 910). If we do not tackle the root causes of homelessness, the number of students experiencing housing instability and in need of services will continue to grow.

Ms. Franklin described other staff that are involved:

We're fortunate here, because we have social workers that will see students. We also have a school social worker that comes one day a

week, which is ludicrous, because we need more time than that. But
they want to work with the special education kids; none of which
my homeless children are. But they will see kids from time to time.

These statements reveal the lack of a structural, stable approach to
ensuring the needs of homeless youth are met within this small school
at Diversey High. McKinney–Vento exists in the legislation and provides
specific provisions to address the social, emotional, and academic needs of
students experiencing homelessness. McKinney–Vento specifically states
that students must have access to the educational and other services they
need to ensure that they have an opportunity to meet the same academic
achievement standards to which all students are held. As uncovered here,
this doesn't necessarily translate into daily routines and practices within
the school building. As outlined in McKinney–Vento, students experiencing homelessness have a right to receive these needed services. Obviously,
these should not negatively impact students with disabilities. However, it
is the responsibility of the school to also provide these services to students
experiencing housing instability.

Lack of funding to support the staff designated to serve homeless students also plays a role in poor policy implementation. The position of
liaison is not accompanied by additional time and pay. It is an additional
responsibility without pay. Ms. Franklin shares that she is required to
attend trainings every year but is not compensated for her time. Funding
limitations are an area that should be addressed when considering appropriate implementation of McKinney–Vento.

Regarding the connection between homelessness and race, Ms. Franklin (who identifies as African American) states:

I think it's a complicated thing. I think that often African Americans
are homeless. It's like there's nobody for you to stay with. I think
that for Hispanics, particularly Mexican Americans, doubling-up
is much more common; . . . the family is extended, my cousins,
my aunt, people just kinda live together. It used to be like that in
the African American community, but it's become so fragmented
in the last I would say 30 to 35 years, that that doesn't happen
anymore. . . . Not only that, but a lot of our children get into these
systems so you know kids that are awaiting placement, kids that
have been thrown away, runaway, and so forth, and that are there on
their own. I feel that in our community there's a disconnect between
adults and children, there's just a disconnect. I think there's been, in
many cases a lot of substance abuse, and there's *always* [emphasis on

always] been a high rate of poverty. Black people ain't got no money, for the most part. It's not like you can go back and you can find a relative that has anything; and it's not that this is across the board, but the people that are in CPS, I know the majority of CPS is Black, I know that, so of course that's gonna make your rates go up.

Here the liaison recognizes the complexity of the various family dynamics experienced by African Americans as well as Hispanics. Her comment addresses the loss of connections youth have to stable adults in their lives, limiting support for their overall development. These remarks also speak to the historical vestiges of race and racism that limited capital and wealth for many African Americans. These limitations are systemic. Race continues to play a role in individuals' access to housing, education, and employment (Hughes & Berry, 2012; Roscigno, Karafin, & Tester, 2009). Recognizing systemic inequities allows for an examination of the ways in which race and homelessness are interconnected.

The media also contributes to society's racial dynamics. Ms. Franklin addresses these racial formations (Omi & Winant, 1994) and perceptions:

Sometimes I think that it's a conscious decision that someone has made, and I mean that "they" [larger society and systems] have made to keep us [African Americans] in the same position. Because your youth are really your future, and then what you are going to become. And if this is all that they know about themselves, and they believe that this is the way that they are, then they're gonna act that way. Nowadays, it's like, oh well, they sit there and they're jiving and they're fooling around and there are some [positive] images, but there are a whole lot of negative images. And I know kids, little kids, little brown kids, if they have a choice they're not going to watch the news, they're not gonna watch the highbrow shows or even the sitcoms that require you to use your brain; they're gonna watch the [music] videos, that's what they watch, and so they're being indoctrinated with this stuff through their eyes and their ears and they believe in all this.

Ms. Franklin's statement identifies the larger social and structural components of race in U.S. society. Focusing her attention on the role media plays in Black youth's perception of themselves, their families, and communities, she recognizes the negative images African American youth are exposed to through various media, specifically hip-hop, as referenced in her comment about young children choosing to watch music videos.

Although there may have been negative portrayals of Blacks in society during her adolescence, there are components to her statement that ring true. For instance, during the late 1960s and 1970s the portrayal of Blacks in mainstream media included James Brown's hit song *I'm Black and I'm Proud* (1968), representative of a larger Black Power movement, opening the door for positive Black images in society. However, this also allowed for the commodification and exploitation of Black images. In the 1970s we start to see characters like Foxy Brown, Cleopatra Jones, and Shaft. On the surface these images are viewed as "positive" within the Black community as these characters are the hero/heroine of the film; however, upon further examination, these types of films have been referred to as "Blaxploitation" (Dunn, 2008), reifying negative stereotypes of Black men (hypermasculine) and women (oversexualized).

From a CRT perspective, racial characteristics and stereotypes are a normal part of our everyday experience. The social constructionist tenet informs folks of color of their "rightful" place in society. Knowing African Americans are overrepresented among homeless students does not cause concern or alarm among the research participants; it is simply "the way things are." This social outlook speaks to the reification of racial hierarchies that exists in institutions of education and the greater United States.

GRAND HIGH

Grand High is an open enrollment school located in an African American neighborhood. Not surprisingly, the student population of Grand High is predominantly African American. Although the average ACT score earned by students is well below average, Grand High has a focused effort to improve the academic rigor of its school, promoting college and academic success for all of its students.

Staff, Climate, and Culture

The halls of Grand High are peppered with encouraging posters that read: "College IS possible!," "We are a school where staff and students excel; parents and community care," "It's all about you—Respect, Honesty, Attitude, Leadership, Caring, Fairness, Tolerance." As Mr. Grant, the assistant principal of Grand High, provides a tour of the school, he shares that due to recent school closings, Grand became a "receiving" school, which has increased their student body over the last few years. He refers to Grand as the Statue of Liberty: "Give us your poor, tired, unwanted" (fieldnotes, November 27, 2007). This has also led to increased tensions among the student body because students have to traverse neighborhoods representing various gangs. He goes on to share that many of the students attending Grand High have no place else to go. Recognizing the complex situations Grand High students experience, the school has applied for and received several programs and grants, including the AVID (Advancement Via Individual Determination) program and partnerships with the Gates Foundation, Illinois Institute of Technology, and the Kaplan Foundation.

While I did not work closely with Mr. Grant in any official capacity, I would regularly see him in the hallways directing students to their classrooms, expediting their transition between classes. He also would spend a couple of periods a day in the lunchroom, enhancing his relationship with students through academic support in the form of tutoring or via informal conversations. This also allowed him to stay abreast of events occurring in the many informal school spaces.

On occasion, students would demonstrate outright disrespect of school staff (swearing or yelling at teachers or other personnel). There were instances in these situations in which the outburst of the student was so disruptive, staff would make their way into the hallway to see what the commotion was all about. On one of these occasions, I could hear a male voice yelling expletives: "Don't put your hands on me! Fuck that! This is some bullshit: you don't have a right to put your hands on me!" After the altercation subsided, Ms. Williams, a member of the Grand High administrative staff, came back in the office, stating, "That's messed up; that wasn't one of the kids, that was an adult, one of the security guards." (fieldnotes, February 28, 2008). It was not uncommon to hear adults yelling at students for rule infractions, demanding they get out of the hallway (after the bell rang indicating the start of class), asking students to remove their hat or coat, or reprimanding them for their conduct, which was the case for this security guard. He was reprimanding a student and the student pushed back. To support security staff at Grand High in monitoring student activity, the school provided them with disposable hand cameras to "catch inappropriate student behavior" on the school premises or school campus grounds (fieldnotes, November 26, 2007). These events are all examples of the ways in which students at Grand High are controlled and disciplined in a setting that should be promoting and facilitating educational endeavors and achievement. The discipline approach is specific to settings and spaces containing large numbers of African American youth in which youth are treated like criminals yet expected to conduct themselves as students.

Ms. Gray

Ms. Gray has worked at Grand High in the capacity of counselor for over 8 years and has been in the role of homeless liaison for over 3 years. Ms. Gray was extremely generous with her time. Although she seemed incessantly occupied, this would seldom discourage her from our interactions. Ms. Gray was exceptionally efficient with multitasking, as she would often have a student in her office as she filled out paperwork, answered her phone, provided information to her colleagues, and supervised her social work intern, Ms. Carey. Students were constantly barraging her with questions, requests, or quick check-ins to say "hello." Ms. Gray noted the large number of homeless students enrolled and identified at Grand High. However, of the 70 plus homeless students, fewer than five met the criteria of unaccompanied homeless youth. On a few occasions she introduced me to a student, and as I engaged the student in the recruitment process, I would learn that they were in the care of a parent or legal guardian. This limited the number of students eligible to participate in the research project.

Ms. Gray is aware of her basic roles and responsibilities as homeless liaison. McKinney–Vento requires that homeless liaisons attend training sessions yearly, as well as conduct a training in which they share this information with the entire school staff. She shared ways in which CPS ensured this knowledge was provided to her:

> Every year you know, we have to go for a refresher at the beginning of the school year, and very little changes have been made in the 3 years. If a parent or a child comes in and says that they're living in a shelter, or they're homeless because of a fire, eviction, or something to that effect, they're doubled-up with family members. I don't ask any questions, especially if they come in to register and if they don't have any records or anything like that. I don't ask any questions, just go ahead and enroll them, and then I find out where they're living. If it is in a shelter, I would like to have, they usually give me something, a statement or some kind of form that says they are indeed living in a shelter. Then I sign them up for the free bus cards and then there you go. Other than that, that's pretty much all that I do with them.

Ms. Gray's overview demonstrates that McKinney–Vento is being minimally implemented at Grand High. As outlined in the legislation, students also have the right to tutoring services and referrals for their subsistence, physical, and mental health needs; however, they do not receive these referrals or support from Grand High, an indicator of the limitation of McKinney–Vento in this particular school setting. Limited time and resources severely impact her reach. She works to ensure that basic provisions of McKinney–Vento are adhered to; however, they are not always given priority or importance. Further, there are several unmet needs (e.g., counseling and tutoring). Ms. Gray shares:

> At the beginning of the school year, after I go to the refresher course, I bring something back, especially if there's new information, which there rarely is. But there's a video that we are required to show, especially to new staff members, to make sure that they're aware of what to look for if a child says that they're sleeping in a car, or if something's going on, they're not at their primary residence. . . . It's required that everybody views the video, and then gives their opinion, you know Q & A session, but that's pretty much it. This usually occurs during the first three days right before school starts. There's all kinds of new information that may come about. There's information that the staff are required to know, and if the principal has 20 minutes that she wants to fill, that's where I come in (laughs). . . . It should be a priority, but no, it's not, and to a degree it depends on the principal. The former principal you know she made sure that I had time to talk about the issue, but this principal doesn't.

This comment speaks to people's perceptions of its importance. How policy is implemented is contingent on the school leadership, which also influences the importance, urgency, and capacity of liaisons. The approach taken by Grand High also demonstrates the lack of structure in place by the larger school district to ensure that liaisons are provided the support needed to properly implement McKinney–Vento. Ms. Gray shared the ways in which school leaders can support or limit the services students receive, for example, in the case of Leon, a student who had been living on the streets in an abandoned building. He had been getting clothing from the school and had been allowed to bathe in the locker room. Then that came to a stop. I asked whether she could have an intervention role in situations like that, and she responded:

> The thing that upset me was that, about that situation, is that the principal stopped it. I mean, he was getting clothes all the time, somebody was always bringing him clothes, shoes, and things

like that, even the kids were doing it. But he ends up leaving it
somewhere or selling it or something like that. It was nice that he
was able to come to school and get a shower, you know he was able
to shower up and things like that. But the principal put a stop to it,
so I don't know.

Asked about the principal's reason, Ms. Gray reported, "She said
'we're not a social service agency.'"

In this situation Ms. Gray felt that she had no discretion to remind
the principal that as a homeless student, Leon should be provided with
this support. She felt that she had no authority to ensure that the student was able to receive services from the school. Although provisions in
McKinney–Vento mandate that students be provided with the service or
referral to the service, the student's access to these services was left to the
charitable acts of the school staff and students. Rather than relying on the
policy to guarantee students the services they require (e.g., referrals), it is
left to the adults—in this case, the principal and liaison—to decide, often
unilaterally. This also illustrates Ms. Gray's lack of awareness, knowledge,
interest, or time to connect students to services related to their self-care.

While homeless educational legislation in Illinois mandates that all
schools have a homeless liaison, the guidelines driving this position are
vague. And perhaps more importantly there is no protection from, or safe
recourse for, a principal who unilaterally decides to withdraw services
in support of homeless students' education. This principal's disregard for
the law seems particularly egregious at a school that promotes itself as a
caring community, dedicated to having all of its students go on to college.
Further, it highlights the lack of awareness, structure, and accountability needed to ensure that the rights and services of students experiencing
instability are enforced. The lack of structure and support provided to
liaisons is illustrated as Ms. Gray shares her experiences with becoming
the homeless liaison for Grand High:

The principal came to me one day and said, "You're going to be the
homeless liaison (laughing)," so that's how I got it.
    "You're going to be the homeless liaison, you're going to go to
this training," that's what she said. "I need you to go to this training
because I need you to be the homeless liaison."

Although the principal had designated her as liaison, she did not feel
qualified to take on that responsibility. She received a half-day training
with the homeless education program.

One of the coordinators and that's who I worked with, and still, to this day, she's my main contact. She is a homeless education program coordinator, from out of the area, our school area.

Illinois created its own legislation to address the needs of students experiencing homelessness (Illinois Education for Homeless Children Act, 1994). This provision differs from the federal legislation in that all schools in CPS must have a designated liaison. Despite this effort, without specific guidelines to serve as parameters for the position's qualifications, it is at the principals' discretion to appoint a homeless liaison for their respective schools.

Given the many needs of the homeless student population within CPS, accountability and support are critical. The lack of accountability measures implemented, especially for individuals who lack experience working with this population, limits the effectiveness of the liaison's role. Therefore, although Ms. Gray made efforts to juggle her many responsibilities, she fell short in her responsibility to provide legally required services to homeless students. Further, as the principal did not see providing services to homeless students as a priority or a legal imperative, Ms. Gray's responsibilities as homeless liaison fell to the wayside without penalty. Instead, it was the homeless students that were penalized, as they did not receive the full range of services McKinney–Vento aims to provide. Aware of her time constraints, Ms. Gray delegated some tasks. For example, she provided the clerk in the main office with a list of students to receive fare cards for transportation. Students would line up at the end of the school day to obtain these fare cards (fieldnotes, January 8, 2008). This speaks to Ms. Gray's efforts to meet the transportation needs of homeless students, though none of their other needs.

When asked if the school provided sufficient time to support her responsibilities as homeless liaison, Ms. Gray responded:

No, I don't because part of the counseling includes one-on-one counseling. I don't have time to do that. I really don't. Once I get into the office, the kids are starving for attention, and I can't give it to everybody, I just can't. Sometimes I feel like once they attach themselves to you, they hold you real tight. And I let that happen when I first came here, 'cause I was excited, you know, to be there. I was excited to be working with the kids. It's something I always wanted to do; but I found you can't do it. You have to have boundaries. You have to hold some of these kids at arm's length, because if you don't, they'll hold onto you and choke you for dear life. . . . But the one thing I'd like to be able to do at some point, would have liked to be able to do, was to offer one-on-one counseling; but then too, CPS doesn't like that, doesn't like the counselors to do career counseling, college counseling, what do you need to get from freshman year to senior year, in a 4-year timely manner. That's all they want counselors to do, you know doing test preparation, facilitating standardized tests; other than that, counseling? No!

Lack of structural support from Grand High and the larger CPS structure increases the likelihood that students will not receive needed services. Ms. Gray also highlights the reality that the primary concern of schools within CPS is test scores; a focus that often impedes meeting student's social–emotional needs. This reality reflects NCLB policies that focus on test scores, which often supersede other legal mandates such as the provisions outlined in McKinney–Vento. Again, this conundrum is not isolated to the CPS system. It is a reflection of the larger educational landscape in which testing dominates and drives school instruction and preparation (Kohn, 2000).

While discussing homeless students in the larger CPS context, Ms. Gray is astonished at the large number of students experiencing homelessness (over 10,000 during the 2007–2008 school year). Viewing Ms. Gray's insights from a CRT perspective reveals the relegation of certain racial characteristics and stereotypes embedded in the larger social context. Similar to the perspectives of the other liaisons and students who participated in this project, the social constructionist tenet informs folks of color of their "rightful" place in society. While she is surprised at the large amount of students experiencing homelessness, the fact that 90% of the students are African American does not cause concern or alarm for Ms. Gray. It is simply "the way things are." This understanding speaks to the reification of racial hierarchies that exist in institutions of education and the larger U.S. society.

ADMINISTRATORS AND ADVOCATES

Ms. Jones

Interviews and interactions with school staff provided a broad understanding of the context in which unaccompanied students of color experiencing homelessness functioned in the respective school contexts. Ms.

Jones, the director of the district's homeless education program, shared her experiences, perspectives, and insights regarding access and services for homeless students.

According to Ms. Jones, the homeless education program has a total of seven staff, four at central office and three in the field. The staff in the field are responsible for outreach, monitoring, and compliance:

> They're [program staff] each responsible for two clusters or about 200 schools apiece, so they do a lot of trouble shooting. They help with enrollment issues. They help with allegations of fraud. If there's a school that says, I think that this family isn't really homeless, or they already live in our attendance area and they're just claiming homeless in order to get into our school, they help with those. They also help with visiting shelters, making sure all the kids at the shelters are participating in school programs, and then also work to get preschool kids enrolled, because that's an initiative too—that we need to try and make sure all of the little ones are enrolled, so that as they go along, they get a head start. Then they can do a little better in school and hopefully their academics will stay fairly stable through high school.

As Ms. Jones notes, one person is responsible for monitoring 200 schools for McKinney–Vento compliance over a 10-month period. This allows staff to spend, at best, approximately one and a half days at each school per academic year. How effectively can schools be monitored considering the 1:200 ratio? This ratio highlights the lack of structure in place to monitor accountability and compliance of McKinney–Vento enforcement in the district. The personnel structure of CPS's homeless education program thus limits to near nonexistence any reliable, timely monitoring of McKinney–Vento. As a result, if a school has significant issues with their compliance, it is up to the student, parent, or school to contact the administrative offices of CPS and report it. CRT allows us to interrogate the ways in which race shapes experiences of students of color identified as homeless. CRT implores us to ask, would the approach be the same if 90% of the homeless student population were White?

Ms. Jones goes on to share information about accountability of individual schools as well as the system as a whole:

> The liaisons and clerks are accountable to the principals, OK, but then we make sure that the principals are complying with what they have to do. . . . The AIOs [Area Instructional Officers] support us in

that, I mean because they're over the principals so that if there's an issue, usually principals eventually comply.

This would mean that with about 600 schools in CPS, Ms. Jones and her staff of seven are responsible for all the schools. She elaborates:

Yeah, we're responsible for making sure that schools comply with the McKinney–Vento Act, but we get support from CPS, because they understand that it's federal law, and they're mandated.

We have the state coordinator and they support us too. I mean the state homeless act is pretty much word for word the McKinney, maybe even a little bit more, stronger maybe, so there's both laws and of course CPS policies too.

And technically CPS could lose funding, if they weren't compliant.

In addition to the measures taken by CPS related to monitoring and compliance, Ms. Jones meets with a lawyer from the homeless advocate agency that brought a suit against CPS for prior noncompliance to discuss ways in which to address any issues of noncompliance (Ms. Jones, personal communication, April 11, 2008; Ms. Davis, personal communication, July 11, 2008). As noted above, there are mechanisms in place to assure compliance; however, it is up to individual personnel at individual schools to ensure mandates are being followed and to report persons or schools not in compliance.

Ms. Jones also recognizes that McKinney–Vento legislation does not contain specific requirements in regard to appointing a homeless liaison. She shares her opinion of the qualities homeless liaisons should possess:

We ask the principal to please look for someone who communicates well, who has compassion for people, doesn't mind giving extra time—because it's extra time with no additional pay—for homeless kids. In some schools we have some really great people. That's not always across the board. But most of the liaisons and clerks are very compassionate and understanding, and they keep things confidential and are really out there to help the students. And that's what we need—someone who's going to be there to help the students and the families. If they have a question, they'll call; they'll either call us or call the liaisons in the field, and we'll try to hook them up with the appropriate assistance.

As illustrated above, Ms. Jones has identified qualities that homeless liaisons should embody. However, McKinney–Vento, at the state and federal levels, does not specifically outline the qualities and/or criteria individuals serving homeless students are required to have. While her approach is admirable, persons should be "compassionate . . . there to help the students," this framing has charitable undertones to it. If people "don't mind giving additional time without additional pay," they may be committed to students, but this does not necessarily mean that school personnel have the skills, tools, and understanding, or the assertiveness or sense of advocacy, required to adequately connect students to the resources and services that will support their educational and individual needs.

The theme of charity was woven into several aspects of discourse connected to homeless student services and needs. Ms. Jones explains that her program also provides school supplies, uniforms, and other basic needs for students:

And we get a lot of different donations and then we try and share those with schools and shelters. We had some books donated so we send those out to shelters and schools. We've been working with Feed the Children, and they've had backpacks and school supplies, and we sent all those out. And we have some bags for younger children, preschoolers, and we're going to be sending all those out. So anything that we have, is donated as far as homeless families. We try to get those out, to anywhere we can in the system, to where there's kids. We have a warehouse and at the warehouse they do a great job of sending these things out to the schools and the shelters. They have kind of like an internal mail system, and so we can get things out to the schools fairly quickly and out to the shelters fairly quickly; they're great.

While the generosity of others is laudable, it does not guarantee that students experiencing homelessness receive their rights to basic resources needed for their role as student, and as guaranteed them under McKinney–Vento. What about the schools and shelters who aren't privileged enough to have these donations shared with them? Moreover, what would the outcome be if these organizations and individuals ceased their donations? The language of McKinney–Vento does not reflect this approach to providing students with their basic educational needs. McKinney–Vento is the result of families and students standing up for their rights. A charitable approach to understanding McKinney–Vento undermines the policy as well as student and family rights.

Similar to other respondents, when asked specifically about the role of race as it pertains to the racial composition of homeless students, Ms. Jones did not specifically address it. However, she did highlight a portion of the homeless student population that is often "hidden" from public view:

> Our Hispanic families are very underreported. That has to do with the fact that they don't identify as homeless even if they're doubled-up; 'cause they figure, they've got a place to live so, I think most of our families, I think it's more cultural. We're trying to do more outreach in the communities regarding Hispanic families, [letting families know] that services are available for the children. But in my own opinion I think it's also the name of the program. I think we need to do something about the name of the program, either call it McKinney–Vento services or Families in Transition, something like that, because of the stigma of the word *homeless*; in Spanish the word is *desamparado*, which means "without life" and that's a real, like you don't have a soul or something like that. That's not what we're trying to do here is have people feel despair; we're trying to give services to help the children, so we might have to do something about the name. We've talked about it for a while, but we haven't officially decided what to do. We have a lot of things on it, with that name on it, and we'd have to change and do a whole different type of campaign and that kind of thing. We might do it like Families and Transition/homeless education; who knows, we'll have to see. I'm not sure, I don't know, maybe McKinney–Vento. Problem with that is that people might not know what it is.

This recognition is important in providing services to the Latina/o student population experiencing housing instability in CPS. Subsequently, CPS changed the name of the program to Students in Temporary Living Situations (STLS). This name better reflects the unstable housing situations many students and families experience. Many homeless advocates and scholars describe the Latina/o homeless population as "hidden" because they often reside doubled- or tripled-up with families and friends, avoiding the public shelter system. Lack of contact with public systems for assistance among the Latina/o homeless population due to issues of citizenship and language keeps them hidden from public view and undercounted (Conroy & Heer, 2003). I also found this to be true, as I was unable to interview Latina/o youth for this project. At Diversey High, of the 44 homeless students, four were Latina/o. Of these four, only one student was unaccompanied, and his lack of attendance prevented his participation in this research. It is important to highlight the Latina/o homeless population—further inquiry and support is sorely needed for this subpopulation of students experiencing instability—however, Ms. Jones's response falls short of a more critical analysis of the overrepresentation of African Americans that comprise the homeless student population. Again, race is a dynamic that should be acknowledged and addressed, as it influences how students are perceived, engaged, and treated by school personnel.

Ms. Davis

Ms. Davis is a longtime advocate of homeless families, having worked in the area of poverty and law for well over 2 decades. Ms. Davis led the charge against CPS for their noncompliance in the early 1990s. As a result of these efforts, she has become an integral part of the monitoring and compliance of McKinney–Vento implementation in the CPS system.

Ms. Davis shares her insights on the significant impact adults can have on the lives of unaccompanied homeless youth:

> Really, I think many of us who work in the advocacy community with homeless youth feel that one persistent caring adult in the life of a child can certainly make a big difference—keep them in school, keep them on a better path, help them assimilate, adapt to or accommodate the trauma without becoming dysfunctional. You link them up with a tutoring program, or you help them with some of those expenses. You build a personal relationship with them. You can definitely recover those kids and then getting them the credit they deserve . . . you know you could make a good student out of them. I mean on our board is a young woman who was a bad student the first two years of high school. She got in a lot of trouble and couldn't have cared less. One single caring person who really got her to focus on what her education might mean changed her life. And now she's graduated from a top tier university law school and works for a well-known law firm here in Illinois. I think the lack of any adult following them or showing concern for them is a problem.

Her statement is significant to McKinney–Vento as it demonstrates the positive outcomes that can come about as a result of a youth's connection to a caring adult in their lives. For schools, this means creating opportunities for students to make connections, continually building on these to provide guidance and support to students that lack this structure in their homes. The experiences of the unaccompanied homeless students at Diversey High speak to this notion of connectedness. John and Jack received significant support from teachers and counselors, allowing them to feel good about their educational experiences and maintain their attendance. Conversely, Natalie expressed her frustration at the lack of adult concern, resulting in her departure from school.

Ms. Davis shared her perspectives on why many unaccompanied homeless students do not receive the services and support outlined in McKinney–Vento:

> Well, in Chicago, overwhelmingly the children experiencing homelessness are African American, and next to that are Latino children. So in our community it is undeniably an issue of race. My experience is that there seems to be, I think, lesser expectations of children of color often. I think there seems to be an identification particularly of the males that they are problematic and they need to be disciplined and controlled. I think there's systemically not much compassion shown to these kids, and I think all those aspects have a racial dimension to them. I also feel, I think human rights reflects, I really don't care if people possess intentional racial animus against people of color, but I think when you look at what happens to people of color and you see how much they don't get and the degrading situations they are placed in in the school system, that in and of itself is a racist issue from my perspective. Every one of these children should get more than they are getting now. Why do we have a school system where we know there's a gap in achievement? We know things that work to address that gap in achievement, we know what's required, and we consistently don't provide it.

When asked to further explain or illustrate ways in which she feels CPS as a system has racial undertones to it she shared:

> Absolutely, all the Ren2010 schools, all the kids who were pushed out and moved around due to Ren2010 without any regard for what would happen to their learning were all children of color, and until we filed our motion in that context to try to stop the harmful effect of Ren2010, there was no attention whatsoever being paid to the fact that these children had moved three, four, five times. Public housing

had come down, they'd become homeless, they were moving every time something different was being torn down: that is a racial issue. That's not happening to White folks . . . they're not being valued in the same way. Do you think there would be a Ren2010 in Wilmette [affluent White suburb of Chicago]? No, there would not be.

Ms. Davis recognizes and addresses the unspoken racial manifestations of CPS initiatives and policies that disproportionately impact students of color. As in Peggy McIntosh's seminal essay "White Privilege: Unpacking the Invisible Knapsack" (1989), Ms. Davis identifies the "package of unearned assets" Whites accrue due to their racial status, pointing out that these educational injustices are "not happening to White folks." Further, she recognizes the systemic "intentional racial animus" against students of color, placing the onus on the school system as a whole, not on particular individuals. A structural racism approach acknowledges that systemic racism is much more powerful in explaining racial dynamics than focusing on individual acts. The teachers, administrators, and staff Ms. Davis refers to in CPS reflect the structural racism occurring in schools. It is not their individual acts that limit access for unaccompanied homeless youth of color, but the larger system that views students of color in a particular way. As illustrated by the comments, approaches, and perceptions of the adults who engaged in this research, racial systems mitigate the experiences of students of color identified as homeless. It is apparent that several adults interviewed and observed for this project are sincere in their efforts to support students experiencing homelessness. However, their efforts are dulled by a school system and structure shaped by race, and by their evident lack of a sense of their own efficacy to help students receive legally mandated services, which in turn undercuts their efforts to even try.

CHAPTER 4

Moving Toward Justice

I speak not for myself but for those without voice . . . those who have fought for their rights . . . their right to live in peace, their right to be treated with dignity, their right to equality of opportunity, their right to be educated.

—Malala Yousafzai, speech to the UN General Assembly, July 2013

McKinney–Vento functions within the United States, a social system in which there exists systemic inequities of race, class, gender, sexuality, ability, language, age, and a host of other social status indicators. Consequently, McKinney–Vento policy is subject to interpretation and implementation within said systemic inequities. A multifaceted approach is needed to facilitate and promote educational access and better educational and life outcomes for unstably housed youth of color. Youth experiencing housing instability and the adults implementing and enforcing McKinney–Vento are integral to this conversation. A critical component of this work is the understanding that the youth experiencing housing instability are the experts and should be included in the development and implementation of McKinney–Vento reforms. Additionally, the input of teachers, students, families, and other community agencies working with unaccompanied youth experiencing housing instability is fundamental to the continued quest for ensuring students access and enforcement of their educational rights. CRT promotes the centering of voices that are too often marginalized. Soliciting, honoring, and respecting the voices of unstably housed youth encourages the identification of practical needs such as counseling to support their emotional needs, a broader/more complex framing of *homelessness* that better describes their experiences with instability, an understanding of the ways in which the policy functions in school, and, most importantly, actions that support youth while collaboratively working to eradicate youth homelessness. These insights illuminate students' experiences with, and access to, educational institutions and the ways in which their educational rights are infringed upon. It is these insights that guide the suggestions for addressing the educational rights of unstably housed youth of color. This chapter provides suggestions that aim to create stronger structures and systems that will positively shape the educational experiences of youth experiencing instability, simultaneously facilitating awareness and access to their educational rights.

The suggestions are organized into three areas: policy, schools, and society; however, it should be noted that these areas maintain a fluid and reciprocal relationship, each influencing the other. Therefore, the long-term success of one area is contingent on what is occurring within other areas.

POLICY IMPLICATIONS

The perspectives and experiences shared by youth experiencing housing instability and the adults that engage with these youth provide a glimpse into factors and dynamics that shape their involvement with public policy. Hearing from the youth themselves highlights the complexity of their experiences, simultaneously illuminating McKinney–Vento's strengths and limitations. Three main areas of concern include (1) vague language/criteria in the appointment of homeless liaisons; (2) weak systems of accountability at the federal, state, and school levels; and (3) insufficient funding.

More Specific Criteria/Language

While McKinney–Vento does have specific language in regard to eligibility for services, types of services, and support to be provided and dispute resolutions processes, McKinney–Vento legislation does not contain specific requirements in regard to appointing a homeless liaison. As shared by the district coordinator, Ms. Jones, principals have the discretion to appoint individuals to the role of homeless liaison, with little to no guidance for the skills, attributes, and dispositions needed to successfully fulfill this role. As Ms. Jones highlights, the district encourages principals to choose individuals who are empathetic to students' plight and are willing to give additional time to servicing students with no monetary compensation. While these attributes are helpful, they do not ensure that the rights of students as outlined in McKinney–Vento will be fulfilled. This approach embodies a charitable structure, rather than one of justice. It is an injustice to students already experiencing instability, emotional turmoil, and marginalization to have their educational rights infringed upon due to a homeless liaison's lack of experience and/or understanding of educational policy. It is crucial that McKinney–Vento adopt more specific criteria to provide states and districts with a concrete set of skills and knowledge required for the role of homeless liaison. As suggested by the students in this study, this should include in-depth experience with mediation, counseling, navigation of social services and systems, cultural competency, and educational policy. These attributes are key for the successful understanding, implementation, and accountability of McKinney–Vento in districts and schools. A description of skills required for the role of homeless liaison must be coupled with increased funding to support individuals serving in this role. Creating specific criteria also allows for increased accountability at the federal, state, district, and school levels to properly oversee and monitor effective implementation of McKinney–Vento by liaisons.

Frames of race and class further our understanding of homeless educational policy and its implementation. According to Soss, Fording, and Schram (2011), "racial group reputations can guide assumptions about target characteristics at either the collective or individual level, and at any stage of the policy process" (p. 78). They also state: "It becomes more likely that racial distinctions will underpin social classifications that guide interpretations and choices in policy settings" (p. 79). As homeless advocate Ms. Davis so poignantly reflected, situations in which youth of color find themselves in urban schools are not occurring to White affluent students. It is the less tangible, subtler structures of race not addressed in homeless education literature or policy that become problematic. Due to the systemic segregation of African American youth in communities and schools, they are subjected to poor facilities, receive few resources, and are "criminalized" by society and the educational institutions they encounter. Many youth of color struggle to attain an education in these environments. The structural racism that exists in society affects students of color experiencing instability on many levels including, but not limited to, school structure, daily racial microaggressions, and overall instability (in home and school). Further, Bonilla-Silva (2006) contests claims made in William Julius Wilson's seminal piece, *The Declining Significance of Race* (1987), particularly "Wilson's main claim—that class rather than race was the central obstacle for Black mobility" (p. 43). Bonilla-Silva contends that this argument falls short in providing a "meaningful explanation of how discrimination affects minorities' life chances" (p. 44) because it lacks a real discussion of the intersection of race, class, and other social identities youth embody.

Incorporating language that explicitly addresses race within McKinney–Vento policy confronts the disproportionate impact of homelessness on students of color. This reflects the recent findings by the Committee to End Racial Discrimination (CERD, 2014), in which the committee "reiterates its previous concern that the definition of racial discrimination used in federal and state legislation, as well as in court practice, is not in line with article 1, paragraph 1 of the Convention, which requires States parties to prohibit and eliminate racial discrimination in all its forms, including practices and legislation that may not be discriminatory in purpose, but are discriminatory in effect" (p. 2). Knowing that youth of color are a significant faction of students being served by McKinney–Vento, it is critical that legislation at both the federal and state levels directly take on the racial by-products of the policy by including explicit racial language. "With this conceptualization of the relationship between race and class—as both cultural and political-economic constructs—critical race theorists can offer a more incisive intervention at the point of analysis and then again at the point of policy intervention" (Dumas, 2013, p. 123).

Stronger Systems of Accountability

Students consistently reported access to transportation; despite some limitations, overall, this is an aspect of McKinney–Vento that is well implemented. Additionally, all students reported regular access to school meals, another component of McKinney–Vento that is working well. The federal McKinney–Vento guidelines do not mandate that every school have a designated liaison charged with providing assistance and services to homeless students; however, the Illinois Education for Homeless Children Act does. The two schools in which this work was conducted both had in place liaisons for their respective schools. Although the liaisons did not implement all components of McKinney–Vento to their fullest capacity, they consistently fulfilled the responsibility of connecting students to meals and transportation. However, students also have the right to tutoring services and referrals for their subsistence, physical, and mental health needs. These important, necessary services were not made available or accessible to the majority of the unstably housed students that participated in this project. As a result, youth did not obtain the required support McKinney–Vento mandates by law.

Increased efficiency regarding McKinney–Vento requires contending with systematic factors that limit awareness, implementation, and enforcement of McKinney–Vento at the school, district, and state levels. Until these structures/systems are in place, real accountability is not likely. Currently, the consequence for lack of proper implementation of McKinney–Vento primarily or solely impacts students—they are deprived of crucial resources and support.

According to Dr. John McLaughlin, the federal coordinator for the United States Department of Education's Prevention and Intervention Programs for Children and Youth Who are Neglected, Delinquent, or At Risk and the Education for Homeless Children and Youth Program (EHCY), there are no guidelines for homeless student data collection and accountability (McLaughlin & Miller, 2014). The federal government's failure to develop such guidelines prevents youth and families experiencing instability to hold their schools accountable when their rights are violated. As more and more states grapple with how best to meet the needs of students experiencing instability (Miller, 2013), McKinney–Vento becomes muted in its ability to ensure students' rights are met.

Questions of accountability continually arose; students repeatedly informed me they had not been made aware of their rights or access to services (fee waivers, clothing, and so on). Students were able to identify areas listed under student rights that would have been helpful to them during their experiences with housing instability, namely assistance with purchasing school uniforms and supplies, night school fees, general school fees, school enrollment, school participation, and, to a lesser degree, transportation. Without a system of accountability in place, states, schools, and districts most likely will continue to lack programs and practices that ensure student awareness of, and enforcement of, their rights. Practices such as providing a letter or information session to all students during their homeroom period to make them aware of their rights to services set forth by McKinney–Vento could be implemented. Due to confidentiality issues as well as the stigma associated with the term *homelessness*, creating awareness among all students increases the likelihood that more students will be aware of McKinney–Vento policy and, more importantly, the eligibility criteria for seeking out services. As evidenced by the stories of the homeless liaisons, the CPS system is not equipped to provide the many services homeless students require. Forcing students to seek out information places the onus on the youth. McKinney–Vento clearly details the responsibility of districts to create awareness and provide services that support the academic trajectory of unstably housed youth.

Accountability at the federal level coupled with strong systems at the state and district levels is needed to ensure that students' rights under McKinney–Vento are protected. This system can be combined with national strategies for "getting better data" as outlined in the United States

Interagency Council on Homelessness (USICH, 2013) report, *Framework to End Youth Homelessness*. The report outlines several strategies needed to adequately address the needs of youth experiencing housing instability. Specifically, it suggests "Coordinating Federal data systems that collect information on youth experiencing homelessness and their receipt of services" (p. 5). Including educational data within this system allows for the monitoring of services youth receive at the school and district level, sanctioning improved compliance and accountability—improvements that can make the difference between a student remaining and graduating from high school or being pushed out.

Further, legislators recognized that "[McKinney] is an essential first step towards establishing a national agenda for action to eradicate homelessness in America. . . . No one in this body should believe that the legislation we begin considering today is anything more than a first step towards reversing the record increase in homelessness" (Congressional Record, p. S3683, March 23, 1987, as cited in NCH, 2006). With this recognition, and the continued rise of students and families experiencing housing instability, it is essential that more be done to ensure schools, districts, and others receive support/resources, while simultaneously developing stronger policy systems that mandate accountability.

Increased Funding

As noted by the CPS district administrator, Ms. Jones, the majority of McKinney–Vento funding provided to CPS is spent on transportation, leaving little for the many other needs of students experiencing instability. Therefore, such pressing needs (e.g., clothing, school supplies, and mental health services) of unstably housed students are obtained through donations received at the administrative level and then sent out to individual schools. McKinney–Vento covers mandatory school fees, as well as some extracurricular costs. Although most school fees and school-related costs are covered, this is not inclusive of the variety of events offered to the general student population, such as costs associated with prom or yearbooks (fieldnotes, May 5, 2008). Although teachers, principals, and staff may not deem these events important, for many students at the high school level, the ability to participate in senior prom and obtain a yearbook to be signed by teachers and friends is significant to their overall school experience. Lack of funding for events not regarded as "important enough" by the adults making decisions should be reconsidered in light of their meaning to the students who persistently work for educational success, notwithstanding their experiences with instability. Their fate in being able to participate in school events and activities should not be left in the hands of charity.

During fiscal year 2009 Illinois provided school districts with 3 million dollars to serve homeless students. This funding was of benefit to 36 districts in Illinois, allowing them to provide the following: transportation services; social workers, case managers, and homeless liaisons to deliver support services; the expansion of academic services such as tutoring, summer school, credit recovery, and preschool access; and coordination with community agencies to provide vital social and health services needed such as health, housing, and employment (CCH, 2013b). However, due to the budget deficits faced by Illinois, this funding has not been given priority since 2009, and advocates, students, and their families have been working for its restoration. As noted previously, the current federal funds to support McKinney–Vento are insufficient and must be increased. As demonstrated in Illinois, increasing this funding would provide homeless students with access to critical services.

At the national level, funding for McKinney–Vento's Homeless Assistance Grants is $2.105 billion, which is $301 million dollars below the proposed level (National Alliance to End Homelessness, 2014). By the Alliance's estimates (August 2014), "this funding will **not** (author's emphasis) be enough to cover all renewals and will result in communities needing to once again reduce their capacity to address homelessness. The Senate Appropriations Committee voted in June to provide $2.145 billion for the program, a small $40 million increase that may cover renewals but will in **no way** (author's emphasis) expand our nation's capacity to prevent and end homelessness" (para. 5). Further federal investment is needed to justly make an impact on individuals and families experiencing homelessness. The Obama administration's proposal to modestly increase funding to $2.406 billion should be supported, allowing for the necessary investment in programs to address the needs of individuals experiencing housing instability.

SCHOOLS AS SPACES OF STABILITY, CARE, AND JUSTICE-CENTERED EDUCATION

Schools need to serve as vital spaces of stability and care. All students, regardless of their housing status, learn best when they feel safe, supported, and cared for. The youth interviewed for this project all expressed the desire for more support and care from the adults they encounter daily at school. Tensions with parents or guardians at home spill over into their educational lives, and many unaccompanied youth experiencing housing instability are left feeling as though adults in general don't care. Further support and attention on behalf of caring adults could result in solutions and actions that facilitate better education experiences and outcomes for unstably housed youth, not just in school but in their overall lives. Despite the gains made in creating awareness and facilitating proper implementation of McKinney–Vento in schools, there is still much work to be done.

Murphy and Tobin (2011) note that "[homeless student] success will also be dependent upon the ability of school staff to create a caring and stable culture, both in classrooms and the school as a whole" (p. 244). It is apparent that unstably housed students look to their respective schools for guidance and support during this time of instability. These students continued to view school as critical to their lives and made consistent efforts to sustain enrollment and attendance. For example, Leon initially received support from the school principal, but their relationship became tenuous as Leon's situation continued to worsen, negatively affecting his behavior, schoolwork, and appearance. Therefore, in our early interviews, Leon identified the school principal as someone he felt was supportive; by our last interview, his perception had changed, and he instead viewed the principal as someone who was not at all supportive. These intangible systems of support cannot be mandated or articulated in policy. These relationships can only be fostered through the genuine willingness of adults who care and show unconditional support for youth in these situations.

Justice-centered education promotes classrooms and schools as sites where "young people envision, enact and renew democratic life" (Ayers, Quinn, & Stovall, 2009, p. xiv). Educators must then create conditions that promote and nurture equity. Supporting students in their ability to identify and combat injustices such as homelessness, racism, homophobia, ableism, adultism, and so forth fosters the critical thinking needed to understand the systemic nature of such issues in schools and society. According to Duncan-Andrade and Morrell (2008), approaching education from a critical pedagogical space is essential to addressing inequity:

> For both educator and student, this means discarding the framework of meritocracy and critically embracing the role of the underdog. It means framing a classroom and school culture that utilizes critical pedagogy to critique notions of equal opportunity and access, making education a weapon to name, analyze, deconstruct, and act upon the unequal conditions in urban schools, urban communities, and other disenfranchised communities across the nation and the world. (p. 10)

This approach allows for the development of a citizenry that is engaged, has democratic sensibility, and acts against all forms of inequality.

Schools can (and do) play a role in cultivating awareness and advocacy among students in order to solve real-world problems and promote social change. Further, Hill-Collins (2009) argues for "another kind of public education, one that better prepares the American public for democratic action in our contemporary social and political context" (p. ix).

Race continues to play a role in the manner in which youth are viewed and treated by educational institutions. Too many of our Black and Brown youth have been deemed "disposable" by the numerous institutions with which they come into contact, specifically schools. It is not only their identity as youth that makes them disposable, but their racial and class status as youth of color experiencing homelessness that makes these notions of disposability especially significant (Blackman, 1998; Giroux, 2003). The students that participated in this project have origins in homes and/or communities deemed "dysfunctional" and are therefore viewed by the school system as "deficient." They lack the "proper" social values and norms created by the White majority to be successful in school, and therefore schools tend to focus on setting up compensatory services that will fix the student's "deficiencies" rather than address the systemic inequities that create and perpetuate these hierarchies of race and class. CRT's notion of intersectionality brings to light the multiple identities held by youth experiencing instability and poverty, acknowledging the multiple ways in which they are perceived and discriminated against by school officials. Issues of race, class, gender, sexuality, and adultism were all at play. These perceptions influence the manner in which school officials regard unstably housed youth of color and demonstrate their (un)willingness to implement and enforce educational policies created to improve educational opportunity and access. Noguera (2003) notes:

> A great deal of research on teaching has shown that educators often equate differences (such as in culture, language, or race) with intellectual deficiencies, and that such beliefs often have a profound influence on the expectations that are held toward students. (p. 48)

Lowered expectations by teachers of students of color contribute to complacency among school personnel; therefore, little if anything is done to address issues youth encounter that may have a negative impact on their educational outcomes. Instead, through initiatives such as zero tolerance policies, schools penalize youth. While race and class are the focus of this book, it is important that further work be engaged to explore the ways in which students' gender, sexual identity, citizenship status, or religion affect how they are perceived and regarded by schools and the individuals within them. CRT recognizes that no person has a single, unitary identity. Consequently, exploring the multiplicity of identities youth experiencing housing instability embody serves to illuminate the unique dynamics and interfaces among these various student groups in regard to their treatment in schools and other social institutions.

CRT serves as a catalyst to shift the framework from "deficient" and "disposable" to one that "can re-envision the margins as places empowered by transformative resistance" (Yosso, 2005, p. 70). The strength, tenacity, and resistance of the youth must be recognized and respected. The students demonstrated their resistance in various ways. Sheila refused to subject herself to abuse and as a result left home; Michael recognized the subpar curriculum and lowered expectations the school held, providing a critique of school curriculum, coupled with a refusal to engage in "dumbed-down" curriculum; Natalie acknowledged her teacher's disregard for her privacy as a student experiencing instability and ceased her school attendance. While some may view these behaviors as deviant, they should be seen as acts of resistance; resistance against being treated in ways that undermine one's value and/or neglect one's humanity. CRT recognizes that race and racism are products of a social construction. Research reveals that often young Black males are characterized as "angry" or "hostile" and are perceived by many as a "threat" (Ginwright, 2004; Noguera, 2003). This anger and hostility is not viewed as an indicator of the need for mental health services or counseling due to the students' racial identities. Therefore, teachers and staff make little contact with such students and/or ignore behaviors of "anger" and "hostility," rather than attempting to understand the underlying factors contributing to such actions among these youth. These events and behaviors are written off by several school personnel as students being "disrespectful" or, worse, "just the way they are" (fieldnotes, October 29, 2007, November 5, 2007).

Schools are integral to the communities they serve, having the knowledge, networks, and logistical resources to serve as a hub for the myriad of services needed to provide for the subsistence, educational, and emotional needs of students experiencing instability. Collaboration with community-based organizations (CBOs), mental health clinics, shelters, and the like is a necessary component of creating a large ecosystem of stability, safety, and care to meet students' academic, social, and physical–emotional needs (Miller, 2011; Murphy & Tobin, 2011). Moreover, school coordination with local service agencies or programs is a legal mandate under McKinney–Vento, "(f)The Coordinator for Education of

Homeless Children and Youths established in each State shall . . . (4) facilitate coordination between the State educational agency, the State social services agency, and other agencies (including mental health services) to provide services to homeless children . . . " (NCLB, 2001). The youth who participated in this research would have benefited if coordination with local services had been available at their respective schools: (1) local mental health agencies—Sheila, Leon, Michael, John, Natalie, and Jack would have benefited from seeing an individual or family counselor to process the family dynamics occurring in their lives and their emotional needs; (2) housing programs—Leon, Natalie, and Jack required assistance with housing to provide them access to consistent and safe housing; (3) food and clothing pantries—Jack, Leon, Sheila, and Natalie shared instances or periods of time when they were not able to secure jackets and clothing appropriate for Chicago's inclement weather and within the school's dress code; (4) juvenile justice programs—Natalie, Jack, Michael, John, and Leon would have benefited from legal advice in regard to their individual and family situations; and (5) general life skills and coaching support—all six youth were negotiating adult programs and systems; encouragement, guidance, and advice from a consistent adult(s) could have made a positive impact. Coordination of programs such as these also contributes to the youths' understanding of their housing status, their eligibility for, and their awareness of rights to, programs and services under McKinney–Vento.

During a recent Summit on Youth Homelessness, mental health was a specific "ask" from youth. They identified a need for "access to life coaches and adults who care about them" as a critical need (Chicago Summit on LGBT Youth Homelessness, 2014). Further, youth feel these relationships need to be long-term. Some of the school personnel struggled to provide youth with basic needs as well as support for their mental health needs. Almost always, this support was in the form of charity, preventing long-term, persistent structural changes to the school itself and proper implementation and accountability in regard to McKinney–Vento. Efforts are underway within CPS to educate CPS staff about services available to students experiencing instability. In August of 2013, 1,200 CPS clerks and homeless liaisons participated in a 6-day training that aimed to increase support for youth experiencing instability in CPS (Chicago Alliance, 2014). With sustained training, support, and accountability, such efforts can make a lasting impact. Schools should serve as spaces to identify, explore, and grapple with real-world issues/topics that are relevant to students' lives. With strong systems of support, youth input, and coordination of programs/services, schools have the potential to be critical spaces of hope and transformation for youth experiencing housing instability.

SOCIETAL CONSIDERATIONS

Many of the systemic inequities unearthed in schools are simply a reflection of social inequalities. Hill-Collins (2009) notes, "Because of its history, race has been tightly bundled with the social issues of education and equity in the U.S. context" (p. x). Failure to address the racial, class, and other inequalities that youth of color experiencing instability face significantly hinders their intellectual, emotional, and social progress. The rhetoric of a postracial U.S. society is a fallacy. Youth of color, particularly males, are continually harassed, criminalized, brutalized, and even killed simply due to their existence as Black males. The stories of Oscar Grant, Trayvon Martin, Michael Brown, Eric Garner, John Crawford III, Tamir Rice, Aiyana Stanley-Jones, Rekia Boyd, and countless others is a shameful reminder of the continued legacy of race and racism in U.S. society. Addressing the issue of housing instability among folks of color in this country means we must seriously address the ways in which racial bias and White supremacy inform our everyday thoughts, decisions, and actions, and the subsequent outcomes for youth of color.

As a signatory on the United Nations document, *The Universal Declaration of Human Rights* (1948), the United States recognizes the right to housing as part of the right to an adequate standard of living in Article 25. However, this is not reflected in everyday policies and practices. The National Law Center on Homelessness and Poverty (NLCHP) has documented the ways in which individuals experiencing homelessness are criminalized, discriminated against, and injured by laws and policies that make it "illegal" to complete basic human tasks in public (NLCHP, 2014). For example of the 187 cities surveyed in their report *No Safe Place*, 53% prohibit sitting or lying down in particular public spaces; 43% prohibit sleeping in vehicles, and 57% prohibit camping in particular public spaces (NLCHP, 2014). These inhumane policies have resulted in the incarceration and even death of individuals experiencing housing instability throughout the United States. These policies are not natural; they are developed by people, people who too often do not have experiences with poverty, homelessness, racism, and other forms of discrimination. Therefore, the approaches often used to address homelessness focus on the individual as the problem, instead of the structures and systems (lack of affordable housing, punitive policies, and so on) that create and reproduce racial and class inequalities. Further, for individuals experiencing poverty, punitive policies exacerbate their attempts at stability. For example, defense attorneys in Missouri find that municipalities profit from poor people. These "'poverty violations'—driving with a suspended license, expired plates, expired registration, and failure to provide proof of insurance"—all contribute to an increased financial burden for folks already experiencing financial strains (Balko, 2014).

Rather than criminalizing individuals of color facing housing instability, we must focus on the root causes of homelessness and racism. This begins by creating more affordable housing and ensuring people's access to it; providing all workers with a living wage so they are able to support themselves and their families; reforming and/or eliminating punitive policies that disproportionately impact poor people of color (both financially and socially); and focusing on our commonality as *humans*—race is a socially constructed phenomena. This requires an ideological shift in our understanding of the world and the ways in which we engage individuals that are perceived as "other." A first step at humanizing individuals experiencing instability is to shift the manner in which we name and frame individuals facing a particular experience. For example, in the field of justice studies, rather than saying *ex-convict*, the more humane term is *formerly incarcerated*; in the area of domestic violence, instead of saying *victim*, individuals are referred to as *survivors*; this shift allows for the centering of the individual and a recognition of his or her humanity. The youth in this research did not see themselves as *homeless* due to the stigma often associated with the term. Referring to students' situations, we can broaden and reframe the discourse by placing the student first; rather than saying someone is "homeless," it can be framed as an individual experiencing "housing instability" to better reflect the systemic conditions that place individuals in precarious housing situations. A justice-centered approach serves to name structural inequalities, simultaneously working to change such conditions.

Furthermore, we must understand the disinvestment that has occurred, and continues to occur, in communities of color. Lack of access to basic necessities such as grocery stores, health services, and education is the reality for many youth of color, not only in Chicago, but across the United States. There is a significant amount of literature that documents the continued disinvestment that has occurred by the city of Chicago as well as Chicago Public Schools, negatively impacting students' access to consistent stable housing, schools, and other crucial resources. The prevailing narrative regarding poor youth of color and their families is one of deficit, dysfunction, and blame. Individuals are seen as incapable, ir-responsible, and lazy; they are at fault for their lack of access to afford-able housing, living-wage jobs, and ability to provide for their children. In response to this false narrative, people of color experiencing housing instability are punished for their supposed failures. Soss et al. (2011) note:

> Neoliberal paternalism promises that, by becoming self-disciplined workers, the poor can achieve full societal membership. Their current marginality reflects the fact that they are undisciplined and irresponsible; their work ethic is underde-veloped; their sexuality is unrestrained; and, as a result, their communities are plagued by disorder and pathology. (p. 81)

As demonstrated here, the focus is on the individuals; however, the attention needs to be on the discourse, policies, and practices that contin-ue to create racial, class, and other systems of inequity. It is these systems and subsequent discourses that reify conditions of injustice. Investing in public resources such as schools, community-based organizations, and social service programs are essential steps toward creating strong public systems of support. Handing schools (and other public goods) over to corporations and the private sector further limits individuals' access to these needed services. It is well documented that schools serve as spaces of stability and support for students experiencing housing instability. As a society it is imperative that we reclaim public spaces, hold our public of-ficials accountable for their actions (or inaction), and highlight the many assets youth and communities have to offer in generating solutions to the myriad of issues society as a whole faces. This must occur not only in schools, but in communities at large. Vaught (2011) insightfully declares, "Community-based Critical Race pedagogy could provide the opportu-nity for building collective tools to challenge and alter structures. This pedagogy could be practiced not singularly or even primarily in schools, but in organizations such as the NAACP, in churches, community centers, and informal meeting places" (p. 201). A multidimensional approach is needed in order to change oppressive systems that disenfranchise youth of color experiencing housing instability.

Homelessness and racism are deep-rooted social problems; as a so-ciety, and more specifically as critical race scholars, we must continue to work toward uncovering and addressing the factors that contribute to and reproduce racial, class, and other social inequities. "CRT scholars in education seek to show the inextricable relationship between educational inequity and race . . . [and] challenge commonsense beliefs about people and communities of color that essentially cite cultural practices and poverty as reasons for educational disparities" (Dixson & Lynn, 2013, p. 3). I am hopeful that the stories shared by the participants and the practices/discourses uncovered in their respective schools bear witness to the ways in which race and class intersect, influencing the opportunities and outcomes for students of color experiencing housing instability. This shift in understanding requires that we continue to identify and name inequitable structures and systems while simultaneously honoring and respecting students experiencing instability—promoting a focus on their strengths, resiliency, and potential while concurrently "calling into question schooling practices that perpetuate Whiteness through expectations for student behavior" (Dixson & Lynn, 2013, p. 3).

As Ladson-Billings (2012) shares, "You don't know where the next cure for cancer will come from, you don't know where Bill Gates is sitting, you have no idea where Toni Morrison is, you don't have any clue that Cesar Chavez is sitting there ready to, at some point in his life, lead farm workers, so you have to teach as if they are in that classroom, they're there somewhere." While this statement is directed at teachers, approaching all youth (and people for that matter) from a perspective of potential and worth, regardless of one's role or "place" in society, serves to create conditions of possibility, transformation, and justice. This approach is critical if our society is serious about ensuring that youth of color experiencing instability are afforded educational spaces that provide support and hope, enabling them to reach their fullest potential.

Epilogue

A couple of years after completing my doctoral research, I was driving home and passed a Chicago Police vehicle parked in the middle lane of South Michigan Avenue, blue lights flashing; two officers were speaking with a Black male. As the warm weather had arrived, so too had the increase of police surveillance in which folks of color are continually stopped for a myriad of reasons. I continued on to my destination and after my brief stop, made my way home. As I turned the corner to my condominium located in a three-flat building, I noticed a young Black male sitting in the middle lane of the same street, only a few blocks south of where I had previously seen the stopped police car. Alarmed by this individual sitting casually in the middle of the street, I took a second look and quickly realized I knew him. It was Leon, one of the youth that I worked with at Grand High experiencing housing instability. I called out his name; he looked up. "You shouldn't be in the street, get up!" I exclaimed. Leon slowly stood up, walked over to the sidewalk where I was standing. He remembered me from Grand High. Leon's appearance was unkempt; he seemed a bit confused. I asked him why he was sitting in the street. He shared that he was recently released from an adult mental health facility and had no place to go. He was trying to get train fare to make his way back to a more familiar area of the city where he might be able to locate and possibly stay with family or friends. He was visibly depressed, head down, shoulders slouched, and expressed his distress regarding his recent departure from the in-patient psychiatric hospital. He is the same Black male I passed earlier who was being questioned by the police. Not sure what to do, I asked Leon to sit on the stoop of our building so I could go inside to see if I could find some cash for train fare.

Concerned that Leon might not wait, I rushed up the three flights of stairs and into the house. I grabbed some nonperishables from the cabinet, and the few dollars and change I was able to find between my purse and home. I made my way back downstairs and Leon was still sitting on the front stoop. We talked for a short time about what had been happening since Grand High, and he shared that things had not really improved for him. After leaving Grand High, he had not had much luck with obtaining employment or support for his housing or physical and mental health needs. He explained that he spent a week or so at the psychiatric hospital. His story was difficult to follow. As I asked clarifying questions working to better understand his situation, I realized that his fractured story was likely reflective of his current mental functioning. He expressed some anxiety around getting to his destination, despite having no specific destination to arrive at. I surmised it was more his concern about getting to a place that was more familiar to him, regardless of his housing situation. I directed him toward the closest train station, hopeful he would arrive somewhere that is supportive and safe. As he has no phone or other means of communication, I quickly realized that I had no means of following up with him once we parted ways. Feeling angry, sad, and defeated, I walked back in the building, comprehending the limited agency and support I am able to garner for Leon. This reality weighed heavy on me, reminding me of why it is so critical that the root causes of homelessness be identified and addressed, and that schools be aware of and accountable to McKinney–Vento. Leon, at best, was shortchanged by his educational institution; at worst, placed in a position where his transition to adulthood means even less attention, support, and understanding of his current circumstances, rendering him an adult who will likely be bounced around from hospital to shelter to the street. As a society we are much less empathetic to the plight of adults experiencing homelessness. It is very likely that Leon's experience will render him invisible, another statistic that society ignores most of the year—avoiding eye contact, or any other form of contact, when individuals approach us on the street, expressway ramps, or other public spaces—yet rallies around during the holidays. This chance encounter with Leon solidified for me that the systematic failure to identify and support students while they are still enrolled in school effectively contributes to adult homelessness. How many others have been funneled into similar unstable housing situations?

As a current teacher educator, I take seriously my responsibility in bringing awareness and understanding of McKinney–Vento to future teachers. However, I understand that my reach is limited and there is a need to institute a structure in which all future and current educators are aware of McKinney–Vento and its mandates (Heybach & Aviles de Bradley, 2014). I also know that transformation and hope are possible. After reading and discussing McKinney–Vento in my education courses, students approach me, sharing their personal experiences with homelessness and the complexity of situations that accompany it. Their presence in the classroom, both the college classroom and their future K–12 classroom, illuminate the tenacity and potential of students who encounter situations of housing instability. As outlined in Chapter 4, a critical component of this effort is working to uncover and dismantle oppressive discourses, systems, and structures that inherently place individuals in positions of marginalization. Working with future and current teachers to discover the ways in which our understanding and framing of the world shapes our engagement with others is needed to transform unjust institutional practices, specifically in school spaces.

Efforts to address McKinney–Vento must extend beyond the school setting. Engaging with individuals in various roles, such as lawyers, liaisons, teachers, advocates, parents, and students, provides for such an opportunity. The Illinois McKinney–Vento Network is comprised of a small group of such individuals. Our group aims to (1) bring awareness regarding the pervasiveness of homelessness among students in Chicago as well as across the state of Illinois; (2) advocate for funding at the city and state level; and (3) generate "best practice" documents that can be shared with teachers, administrators, and others working to ensure students experiencing instability are aware of, and have access to, their individual and educational rights. There is still much work to be done, and it is my hope that this book encourages readers to learn more about what can be done—individually, collectively, and systematically—to create a world in which individuals' human right to housing and education is enacted, not discursively, but in tangible, material, and humane ways.

Research Approach

A qualitative approach was used to capture students' experiences in schools. Qualitative research has served as a tool with which to gain insight on the lives of parents, students, teachers, and administrators in schools (Ayers, 1997; Flores-Gonzalez, 2002; Lewis, 2003; Lopez, 2003; Richie, 1996; Valenzuela, 1999). This project contributes to this body of work by engaging students, teachers, administrators, and advocates on their experiences of homelessness (students) and their knowledge and understanding of policies that address education for homeless students (teachers, administrators, advocates). Learning about the perspectives and experiences of these persons serves to provide a rich account of the manner in which education policy plays itself out in the school setting.

SETTING

Schools for this research were sought out based on the following characteristics: serves students in grades 9 through 12, serves predominantly Latina/o and African American students, serves a high percentage of low-income students, and is located in the city of Chicago. School progress report cards were accessed from the Chicago Public Schools website (www.cps.edu) to identify schools that met the above criteria.

Once I gathered school data, I contacted the homeless education program office of CPS. I spoke with the program coordinator to inquire about high schools that had large numbers of homeless students. I was provided with a list of about 12 schools. Of these, I then identified two predominantly Latina/o and two predominantly African American schools to contact for my research project. I then attempted to contact school principals of these schools to obtain their permission to conduct my research in their schools. I provided these principals with a letter of inquiry introducing myself and detailing the aim of the study, as well as a summary of the research proposal, providing details of intended participants and procedures. After sending this information, I followed up with phone calls and visits to the schools.

After several months and numerous attempts to contact school principals and assistant principals, I was finally granted access into Diversey High and Grand High. One school is predominantly African American (referred to as Grand High), while the other is more ethnically diverse (referred to as Diversey High). Both are considered "neighborhood" schools, meaning that students within the school's attendance boundaries are guaranteed entrance. All names of participants and schools have been changed to preserve anonymity. Respondents were given the option to select their own pseudonym; if not I assigned one to them. The gender and race of my primary respondents were maintained, and small changes were made to a few peripheral characters to preserve anonymity. Lastly, details about both schools were modified to also maintain confidentiality.

SAMPLE

Youth

My research design included unaccompanied homeless youth of color aged 15–19 at two high schools in the Chicago Public School system. Being interested in unaccompanied homeless youth of color, I sought to engage youth who were not in the custody of a parent or guardian and who were African American or Latina/o. Youth were identified by the homeless liaison at each school. School liaisons were provided with a script to inform homeless students about the project I was conducting at their school. If students were interested, the liaison then set up a time for me to meet with the student and discuss in more detail the research project. I provided and reviewed the assent/consent form with each youth individually. Parental permission was waived, as youth may have not been in regular contact or have an amicable relationship with their parent/guardian. Permission from the internal review boards of the University of Illinois at Chicago and Chicago Public Schools were obtained for this research.

Recruitment for youth participants relied solely on referral from a school official to minimize issues of privacy and confidentiality. Posting announcements about the research may have inadvertently "outed" homeless students who may not want to be identified by their peers as homeless. Initially, I obtained assent/consent from a total of eight unaccompanied homeless youth of color from both Diversey and Grand High; however, only six of the eight participated, three from each school (see Table A.1).

Table A.1. Youth Participants

Student	Age	Gender	Race	School
John	16	Male	African American	Diversey High
Natalie	16	Female	African American	Diversey High
Jack	17	Male	African American	Diversey High
Michael	15	Male	African American	Grand High
Sheila	18	Female	African American	Grand High
Leon	17	Male	African American	Grand High

A total of six unaccompanied homeless African American youth were interviewed for this research, four males and two females. The requirements for participation were as follows: unaccompanied homeless youth of color attending a Chicago public school, aged 15–19, either male or female. Three participants engaged in three, 1-hour, audiotaped interviews. Two participants participated in three, 1-hour interviews; however, at their request, they were not audiotaped. One participant completed two longer audiotaped interviews, due to constraints of attendance and time. In addition, two students who agreed to participate in the research (two males, one Latino, one African American) did not participate: One student stopped coming to school, while the other maintained contact with a parent and was not allowed to participate. Although both high schools had large numbers of homeless students (upwards of 50), all but 12 students (at both schools combined) were in the custody of a parent or guardian and therefore were not considered unaccompanied.

School Officials and Advocates

Five adults were interviewed for this project (see Table A.2). Participants included one male and four females; two of the females were African American, two were White, and the one male was also White. The school homeless liaisons were one White male and one African American female from Diversey High, and one African American from Grand High. The two White female participants held roles outside of the schools. One was employed for CPS at the administrative level and the other was an advocate/lawyer employed at a nonprofit organization serving homeless individuals within the Chicago area. The school officials and advocates were recruited based on a purposive sample. Purposive sampling involves selection based on the belief that "what goes on" within a particular space is essential to understanding a process or concept (Schwandt, 1997). Therefore, I did not randomly identify adults to interview; rather, I specifically

Table A.2. Adult Participants

Name	Title	Gender	Race
Mr. Riley	Curriculum Coordinator/Homeless Liaison, Diversey High	Male	White
Ms. Franklin	Counselor/Homeless Liaison, Diversey High	Female	African American
Ms. Gray	Counselor/Homeless Liaison, Grand High	Female	African American
Ms. Jones	CPS Administrator	Female	White
Ms. Davis	Lawyer/Advocate	Female	White

identified adults working with homeless youth in the schools as well as in the community.

My initial intention was to also interview adults the youth themselves identified; however, youth did not identify adults in the school that they felt I should speak with. However, I did speak with various school personnel informally throughout my observations at both schools regarding homeless students and the provisions outlined in McKinney–Vento.

Observations

Observations were carried out for approximately eight months in each school. The majority of my time was spent in the curriculum office at Diversey High and attendance office of Grand High but also fluctuated between assisting with teachers' classes and assemblies and running general errands around the school. In an effort to gain access to the participants' daily lives in the school setting, climate and culture were assessed during my observations. Additionally, I attended various assemblies (talent show, Black History Month, half-gown ceremony, school play, and graduation). I also engaged in activities with the youth, helping out in the classroom and attending after-school groups. Conducting observations in the school setting allowed me to delve below surface events and facts, ultimately revealing meanings that might have been missed in large statistical data sets. As in all settings/environments, social actors, such as researchers, often become accustomed to the day-to-day processes. Often, researchers stop asking critical questions about these processes, viewing them as the "norm." Qualitative research lends itself to question these everyday occurrences and the meaning making that comes of them. Therefore, as I became more comfortable with each school setting, I constantly had to problematize routine behaviors and practices occurring in the schools.

Content Analysis

A document analysis was undertaken for this research, in an effort to understand the larger context in which homelessness is framed and discussed. Documentation regarding educational policy for homeless students was reviewed as well as school documents pertaining to homeless students. This consists of policy at the federal level: McKinney–Vento (Pub. L. 100-77, 101 Stat. 525, 42 U.S.C. § 11431-35), as well as revisions to the policy (PL 100-628; PL 101-645; PL 102-550; PL 103-382; PL 103-421; PL 105-220; PL 106-74; PL 106-377; PL 107-110); and state policy: the Illinois Education for Homeless Children Act of 1994 (HB3244) and its amendments (SB 881; SB1931), as well as court documents pertaining to schools in Illinois and Chicago: *Salazar v. Edwards, Illinois Plan for the Education of Homeless Children and Youth Programs, Illinois State Board of Education Data Collection on Education for Homeless Children and Youth Program;* and lastly, federal documentation that monitors McKinney–Vento compliance: *Report to the President and Congress on the Implementation of the Education for Homeless Children and Youth Program Under the McKinney–Vento Homeless Assistance Act.* Additionally, I collected all documents concerning homeless students specific to each school, as well as each school's weekly newsletters, notices sent home, and the like. Documents were reviewed for the themes regarding homelessness definition, demographics, funding, services, and accessibility.

A qualitative research approach offered the tools needed to examine homeless education policy in the school context, providing further insight into policy adherence, implementation, and accountability at the school level. While the stories of the youth are at the center of my inquiry, context assists in understanding the ways in which the larger world has impacted youths' experiences with homelessness and education, with a specific focus on the manner in which race and racism are discussed and/or omitted from homeless education policy and discourse.

Rights of Homeless Students Form

The Chicago Public Schools shall provide an educational environment that treats all students with dignity and respect. Every CPS homeless student shall have equal access to the same free and appropriate educational opportunities as students who are not homeless. This commitment to the educational rights of homeless children, youth, and youth not living with a parent or guardian, applies to all services, programs, and activities provided or made available by the CPS.

A student is considered **"homeless"** if he or she is presently living:

- in a shelter
- sharing housing with relatives or others due to lack of housing
- in a motel/hotel, camping ground, or similar situation due to lack of alternative, adequate housing
- at a train or bus station, park, or in a car
- in an abandoned building
- temporarily housed while awaiting DCFS foster care placement

All Homeless Students Have Rights To:

- **Immediate school enrollment.** A school must immediately enroll students even if they lack health, immunization or school records, proof of guardianship, or proof of residency.
- **Enroll in:**
  - » the school he/she attended when permanently housed (school of origin)
  - » the school in which he/she was last enrolled (school of origin)
  - » any school that non-homeless students living in the same attendance area in which the homeless child or youth is actually living are eligible to attend.

- **Remain** enrolled in his/her selected school for as long as he/she remains homeless or, if the student becomes permanently housed, until the end of the academic year. Academic success is helped when the student remains in the same school.
- **Priority** in certain preschool programs. Parents or guardians are encouraged to seek enrollment in these programs.
- **Participate** in a tutorial-instructional support program, school-related activities, and/or receive other support services.
- **Obtain** information regarding how to get fee waivers, free uniforms, and low-cost or free medical referrals.
- **Transportation services:** A homeless student attending his/her school of origin has a right to transportation to go to and from the school of origin as long as (s)he is homeless or, if the student becomes permanently housed, until the end of the academic year. CPS staff shall inform homeless parents/guardians or youth of transportation services to and from school and school-related activities.

Types of transportation services:

For homeless students:

- CTA transit cards, transfer fares, and if a student is age 12 years or older a CTA riding permit

For parents of homeless students:

- CTA transit cards for a parent/guardian of homeless Pre-K to Grade 6 students to accompany them to/from school

For preschool through 6th grade, alternative transportation such as busing in parental "hardship" situations where documentation is provided. Examples of "hardship" situations are:

- parent employment, job training, or educational program
- mental and/or physical disability
- children need to be transported to/from schools at different locations
- rules of shelter or similar facility will not permit parent/guardian to leave to transport children to/from school

- court order, DCFS, or DCFS contract agent requires activities that do not enable parent/guardian to transport children to/from school
- other good cause why parent/guardian cannot use public transportation to transport children to/from school

Dispute Resolution: If you disagree with school officials about enrollment, transportation or fair treatment of a homeless child or youth, you may file a complaint with the principal. The principal must respond and attempt to resolve it quickly. The principal must refer you to free and low cost legal services to help you, if you wish. During the dispute, the student must be immediately enrolled in the school and provided transportation, until the matter in resolved. The Homeless Education Dispute Resolution Process Form is available at all Chicago Public Schools and offices, including the Homeless Education Program (773) 553-2242.

Every Chicago Public School has a Homeless Education Program Liaison who will assist you in making enrollment and placement decisions, providing notice of any appeal process, and filling out dispute forms. If you have questions about enrollment in school or want more information about the rights of homeless students in the Chicago Public Schools, call the CPS Homeless Education Program at (773) 553-2242 or the Chicago Public Schools at (773) 553-1000. If you want more information about the rights of homeless students in Illinois, call the Illinois State Board of Education at (1-800) 215-6379.

Annotated Resources

Below are resources to support awareness and services/programming regarding housing instability among youth; this list is by no means exhaustive.

Chicago Coalition for the Homeless (CCH) organizes and advocates to prevent and end homelessness, recognizing and believing that housing is a human right in a just society. www.chicagohomeless.org/

Homeless Youth Handbook: Legal Issues and Options: This handbook provides information to help empower youth in understanding their legal rights. www.homelessyouth.org/illinois

National Alliance to End Homelessness (NAEH) works to prevent and end homelessness through improving policy, building capacity and educating opinion leaders. www.endhomelessness.org/

National Association for the Education of Homeless Children and Youth (NAEHCY) is a national membership association dedicated to educational excellence for children and youth experiencing homelessness, which is working to change systems so all children and youth can learn, succeed academically, and achieve their dreams. www.naehcy.org/

National Coalition for the Homeless (NCH) is a national network of people who are currently experiencing or who have experienced homelessness, activists and advocates, community-based and faith-based service providers, and others committed to a single mission: to prevent and end homelessness while ensuring the immediate needs of those experiencing homelessness are met and their civil rights protected. nationalhomeless.org/

Students in Temporary Living Situations (STLS) is the CPS department that services children and youth experiencing housing instability. The goal of the STLS program is to protect the educational rights of students in temporary living situations and to provide services to students and their families. The staff in the Board's STLS Department also addresses barriers to enrollment, transportation, attendance, retention and success for students in temporary living situations. cps.edu/Programs/Pathways_to _success/Pages/StudentsInTemporaryLivingSituations.aspx

The Homestretch is a documentary film that follows three teens in Chicago experiencing homelessness as they fight to stay in school, graduate, and build a future. kartemquin.com/films/the-homestretch

References

Alexander, M. (2010). *The new Jim Crow: Mass incarceration in the age of colorblindness*. New York, NY: The New Press.

American Academy of Pediatrics (AAP). (1996). Healthy needs of homeless children and families. *Pediatrics, 98*(4), 789–791.

Ashdown, D. M., & Bernard, M. E. (2012). Can explicit instruction in social and emotional learning skills benefit the social–emotional development, well-being, and academic achievement of young children? *Early Childhood Education Journal, 39*(6), 397–405.

Aviles, A. (2001). *Life skill assessment needs of unaccompanied homeless adolescents* (Unpublished master's thesis). University of Illinois at Chicago, Chicago, IL.

Aviles, A., & Helfrich, C. H. (2004). Life skill service needs: Perspectives of homeless youth. *Journal of Youth and Adolescence, 33*(4), 331–339.

Aviles de Bradley, A., & Holcomb, A. A. (2014). *Homeless youth of color in Chicago, Illinois: Access denied* [Shadow report submitted to the International Convention on the Elimination of all forms of Racial Discrimination (ICERD)]. Chicago, IL: Unity Parenting and Counseling & Northeastern Illinois University.

Ayers, W. (1997). *A kind and just parent: The children of the juvenile court*. Boston, MA: Beacon Press.

Ayers, W., Quinn, T., & Stovall, D. (2009). *Handbook of social justice in education*. New York, NY: Routledge.

Balko, R. (2014, September 3). How municipalities in St. Louis County, Mo., profit from poverty. *The Washington Post*. Retrieved from www.washingtonpost.com/news/the-watch/wp/2014/09/03/how-st-louis-county-missouri-profits-from-poverty/

Bell, D. (1973). *Race, racism and American law*. Boston, MA: Little, Brown.

Biggar, H. (2001). Homeless children and education: An evaluation of the Stewart B. McKinney Homeless Assistance Act. *Child and Youth Services Review, 23*(12), 941–969.

Blackman, S. (1998). Disposable generation?: An ethnographic study of youth homelessness in Kent. *Youth and Policy, 59*, 38–56.

Bonilla-Silva, E. (2006). *Racism without racists: Color-blind racism and the persistence of racial inequality in the United States* (2nd ed.). New York, NY: Rowman & Littlefield.

Catholic Charities USA. (2008). *Poverty and racism: Overlapping threats to the common good*. Alexandria, VA: Author.

Chicago Alliance. (2014, February). Chicago's Plan 2.0: Semi-annual progress report. Retrieved from www.cityofchicago.org/content/dam/city/depts/fss/supp_info/Homeless/Plan20/Plan20ProgressReportFeb2014.pdf

Chicago Coalition for the Homeless (CCH). (2001). *Youth on the streets and on their own: Youth homelessness in Illinois.* Chicago, IL: Author.

Chicago Coalition for the Homeless (CCH). (2013a). Frequently asked questions about homelessness. Retrieved from www.chicagohomeless.org/faq-studies/

Chicago Coalition for the Homeless (CCH). (2013b). *Funding fact sheet.* Retrieved from www.chicagohomeless.org/wp-content/uploads/2014/06/3M.Homeless. -Ed.Funding.pdf

Chicago Coalition for the Homeless (CCH). (2014, February). *Gaps in educational supports for Illinois homeless students.* Retrieved from www.ctunet.com/media /press-releases/body/Homeless-Ed-Report-for-release.pdf

Chicago Educational Facilities Task Force (CEFTF). (2014, June). *The report of the Illinois General Assembly's Chicago Educational Facilities Task Force 2012– 2013. Findings and recommendations regarding the implementation of IL P.A. 97-0474 and planning for the future of Chicago's public schools.* Chicago, IL: Author.

Chicago Public Schools (CPS). (2008). Freedom of Information Act Request. Office of Communications, April 28, 2008. Chicago, IL: Author.

Chicago Summit on LGBT Youth Homelessness. (2014, May). *Chicago 2014 Homeless LGBT Youth Summit: Dream it, speak it, do it!* Chicago, IL: Author.

Child Welfare League of America & Lambda Legal. (2012). *Working with homeless LGBTQ youth.* Washington, DC, & New York, NY: Authors.

Committee to End Racial Discrimination. (2014, September 25). *Concluding observations on the combined seventh to ninth periodic reports of the United States of America* (CERD/C/USA/CO7-9). New York, NY: United Nations, International Convention on the Elimination of All Forms of Racial Discrimination.

Conroy, S., & Heer, D. (2003). Hidden Hispanic homeless in Los Angeles: The Latino paradox revisited. *Hispanic Journal of Behavioral Sciences, 25*(4), 530–538.

Da Costa Nunez, R. D., Adams, M., & Simonsen-Meehan, A. (2012). *Intergenerational disparities experienced by homeless Black families.* New York, NY: Institute for Children, Poverty and Homelessness. Retrieved from www.icphusa.org/index .asp?page=16&report=91&type=4

Da Costa Nunez, R. D., & Collignon, K. (1999). Communities of learning: A bridge from poverty and homelessness to education and stability. *Journal for Just and Caring Education, 5*(1), 72–87.

Delgado, R., & Stefancic, J. (2001). *Critical race theory: An introduction.* New York, NY: New York University Press.

De Mare, A., & Kelly, K. (Directors). (2014). *The homestretch* [Motion picture]. Chicago, IL: Kartemquin Films.

Dixson, A. D., & Lynn, M. (2013). Introduction. In M. Lynn & A. D. Dixson (Eds.), *Handbook of critical race theory in education* (pp. 1–6). New York, NY: Routledge.

Dixson, A. D., & Rousseau, C. K. (2005). And we are still not saved: Critical race theory in education ten years later. *Race, Ethnicity and Education, 8*(1), 7–27.

Dohrn, B. (1991). *A long way from home: Chicago's homeless children and the schools.* A report prepared for the Legal Assistance Foundation of Chicago. Washington, DC: Race Research Action Council.

Dumas, M. J. (2013). Doing class in critical race analysis in education. In M. Lynn & A. D. Dixson (Eds.), *Handbook of critical race theory in education* (pp. 113–125). New York, NY: Routledge.

Duncan, G. A. (2005). Critical race ethnography in education: Narrative, inequality and the problem of epistemology. *Race, Ethnicity and Education, 8*(1), 93–114.

Duncan-Andrade, J., & Morrell, E. (2008). *The art of critical pedagogy: Possibilities for moving from theory to practice in urban schools.* New York, NY: Peter Lang.

Dunn, S. (2008). *"Baad bitches" and sassy supermamas: Black power action films.* Urbana, IL: University of Illinois Press.

Durlak, J. A., Weissburg, R. P., & Pachan, M. (2010). A meta-analysis of after-school programs that seek to promote personal and social skills in children and adolescents. *American Journal of Community Psychology, 45,* 294–309.

Elster, A. (2008). *Promoting healthy adolescent development: The view through a half-full looking glass.* Retrieved from cme.medscape.com/viewarticle/575415

Ensign, J. (2004). Quality of health care: The views of homeless youth. *Health Services Research, 39*(4), 695–708.

Ensign, J., & Gittelson, J. (1998). Health and access to care: Perspectives of homeless youth in Baltimore City, U.S.A. *Social Science Medicine, 47,* 2087–2099.

Farmer, S., Pulido, I., Konkol, P. J., Phillippo, K., Stovall, D., & Klonsky, M. (2013, March). CReATE research brief on school closures (CReATE Research Brief #5). Retrieved from www.createchicago.org/

Flores-Gonzalez, N. (2002). *School kids, street kids: Identity development in Latino Studies.* New York, NY: Teachers College Press.

Fothergill, A. (2003). The stigma of charity: Gender, class and disaster assistance. *The Sociological Quarterly, 44*(4), 659–680.

Ginwright, S. (2004). *Black in school: Afrocentric reform, urban youth and the promise of Hip-Hop culture.* New York, NY: Teachers College Press.

Giroux, H. (2003). Racial injustice and disposable youth in the age of zero tolerance. *Qualitative Studies in Education, 16*(4), 553–565.

Gotanda, N. (1995). A critique of "our constitution is color-blind." In K. Crenshaw, N. Gotanda, G. Peller, & K. Thomas (Eds.), *Critical race theory: The key writings that formed the movement* (pp. 257–275). New York, NY: The New Press.

Graves, S. L., & Howes, C. (2011). Ethnic differences in social–emotional development in preschool: The impact of teacher child relationships and classroom quality. *School Psychology Quarterly, 26*(3), 202–214.

Hammer, H., Finkelhor, D., & Sedlak, A. (2002, October). Runaway/thrownaway children: National estimates and characteristics. *NISMART (National Incidence Studies of Missing, Abducted, Runaway and Thrownaway Children).* Washington, DC: U.S. Department of Justice, Office of Justice Programs, Office of Juvenile Justice and Delinquency Prevention. Retrieved from www.ncjrs.gov /pdffiles1/ojjdp/196469.pdf

Heybach, J., & Aviles de Bradley, A. (2014). Introduction: Recognizing blind spots in teacher education and cultivating counter-narratives for justice. *Critical Questions in Education (Special Issue—At the Crossroads of Policy and Poverty: A Critical Look at Homelessness, Youth and Education), 5*(3), 137–142. Retrieved from academyforeducationalstudies.org/journals/journal /current-and-past-issues/volume-5-issue-3-special-issue/

Heybach, L. (2000, Fall). Understanding and implementing the educational rights of children without housing. *Public Interest Law Reporter, 5*, 21–29.

Hill-Collins, P. (2009). *Another kind of public education: Race, schools, the media and democratic possibilities.* Boston, MA: Beacon Press.

Hughes, S. A., & Berry, T. (2012). *The evolving significance of race: Living, learning, and teaching.* New York, NY: Peter Lang.

Illinois Education for Homeless Children Act [ILEHC], HB3244, 105 IILSC 45/145, 1994.

Illinois State Board of Education (ISBE). (2013). *Policy of the Illinois State Board of Education on the education of homeless children and youth overview.* Retrieved from www.isbe.net/homeless/pdf/policy.pdf

Institute for Children, Poverty and Homelessness (ICPH). (2013). *The American almanac of family homelessness.* New York, NY: Author. Retrieved from www .icphusa.org/filelibrary/ICPH_Almanac_url%20watermark_ALL.pdf

Joravsky, B. (2013, March 26). Before the schools, Mayor Emanuel closed the clinics. *Chicago Reader, 42*(27). Retrieved from www.chicagoreader.com/chicago /mayor-emanuel-closes-city-mental-health-clinics/Content?oid=9145051

Klein, J., Woods, A., Wilson, K., Prospero, M., Green, J., & Ringwalt, C. (2000). Homeless and runaway youth's access to health care. *Journal of Adolescent Health, 27*(5), 331–339.

Kohn, A. (2000). *The case against standardized testing: Raising the scores, ruining the schools.* Portsmouth, NH: Heinemann.

Ladson-Billings, G. (2012, October 31). *Cultural competency* [Video]. Retrieved from www.youtube.com/watch?v=Mgouex0WSJw

Ladson-Billings, G., & Tate, W. F., IV. (1995). Toward a critical race theory of education. *Teachers College Record, 97*(1), 47–68.

Leonardo, Z. (2003). The agony of school reform: Race, class and the elusive search for social justice. *Educational Researcher, 32*(3), 37–43.

Leonardo, Z. (2012). The race for class: Reflections on a critical raceclass theory of education. *Educational Studies, 48*(5), 427–449.

Lewis, A. (2003). *Race in the schoolyard: Negotiating the color line in classrooms and communities.* New Brunswick, NJ: Rutgers University Press.

Liebow, E. (1993). *Tell them who I am: The lives of homeless women.* New York, NY: Penguin Books.

Lopez, N. (2003). *Hopeful girls, troubled boys: Race and gender disparity in urban education.* New York, NY: Routledge.

Loseke, D. R. (1997). "The whole spirit of modern philanthropy": The construction of the idea of charity, 1912–1992. *Social Problems, 44*(4), 425–444.

Lynn, M. & Dixson, A. D. (Eds.). *Handbook of critical race theory in education.* New York, NY: Routledge.

Markward, M. (1994). Compliance with the McKinney Act: Providing homeless children with educational opportunity. *Social Work in Education, 16*(1), 31–38.

Marullo, S., & Edwards, B. (2000). From charity to justice: The potential of university-community collaboration for social change. *American Behavioral Scientist, 43*(5), 895–912.

Mawhinney-Rhoads, L., & Stahler, G. (2006). Educational policy and reform for homeless students: An overview. *Education and Urban Society, 38*(3), 288–306.

McIntosh, P. (1989, July/August). White privilege: Unpacking the invisible knapsack. *Peace and Freedom: Magazine of the Women's International League for Peace and Freedom*, pp. 10–12.

McKinney Homeless Assistance Act of 1987—see Stewart B. McKinney Homeless Assistance Act of 1987.

McKinney–Vento Homeless Education Improvements Act of 2001—see No Child Left Behind Act of 2001.

McLaughlin, J., & Miller, J. (2014, April). *Schools and communities responding to students experiencing homelessness and high mobility.* Forum held at the Growing Up Homeless Forum, People's Emergency Center, Philadelphia, PA.

Miller, P. M. (2011). A critical analysis of the research on student homelessness. *Review of Educational Research, 81*(3), 308–337.

Miller, P. M. (2012). Educating (more and more) students experiencing homelessness: An analysis of recession-era policy and practice. *Educational Policy, 27*, 805–838.

Mills, C. (2003). *From class to race: Essays in White Marxism and Black radicalism.* Lanham, MD: Rowman & Littlefield.

Milner, H. R. (2012). Understanding urban education from the outside in and inside out. *Urban Education, 47*, 1019–1024.

Milner, H. R. (2013). Analyzing poverty, learning and teaching through a critical race theory lens. *Review of Research in Education, 37*, 1–53.

Murphy, J., & Tobin, K. (2011). *Homelessness comes to school.* Thousand Oaks, CA: Corwin Press.

National Alliance to End Homelessness (NAEH). (2006). Fundamental issues to prevent and end youth homelessness (Youth homelessness series, brief no. 1). Retrieved from http://www.endhomelessness.org/page/-/files/1058_file_youth _brief_one.pdf

National Alliance to End Homelessness (NAEH). (2014). *McKinney–Vento Homeless Assistance Grants.* Retrieved from www.endhomelessness.org/pages /mckinneyvento_HAG

National Center for Homeless Education (NCHE). (1999). Homeless education: An introduction to the issues. Retrieved from center.serve.org/nche/downloads/ briefs/introduction.pdf

National Coalition for the Homeless (NCH). (2005, June). *Education of homeless children and youth* (Fact Sheet #10). Washington, DC: Author.

National Coalition for the Homeless (NCH). (2006, June). *McKinney–Vento Act.* Fact Sheet #18. Washington, DC: Author.

National Law Center on Homelessness and Poverty (NLCHP). (2014). *No safe place: The criminalization of homelessness in U.S. cities.* Washington, DC: Author.

Nieto, S. (1996). *Affirming diversity: The sociopolitical context of multicultural education* (2nd ed.). New York, NY: Longman.

No Child Left Behind Act of 2001, Pub. L. 107-110, Title X, Part C, Sec. 1031ff. (McKinney–Vento Homeless Education Improvements Act of 2001) § 20 U.S.C. 6301, 115 Stat. 1989 (2002).

Noguera, P. (2003). *City schools and the American dream: Reclaiming the promise of public education.* New York, NY: Teachers College Press.

Omi, M., & Winant, H. (1994). *Racial formation in the United States: From the 1960s to the 1980s.* New York, NY: Routledge.

Parker, L., & Lynn, M. (2002). What's race got to do with it? Critical race theory's conflicts with and connections to qualitative research methodology and epistemology. *Qualitative Inquiry, 8*(1), 7–22.

Reid, P. (1999). Young homeless people and service provision. *Health & Social Care in the Community, 7*(1), 17–24.

Richie, B. E. (1996). *Compelled to crime: The gender entrapment of battered Black women.* New York, NY: Routledge.

Roscigno, V. J., Karafin, D. L., & Tester, G. (2009). The complexities and processes of racial housing discrimination. *Social Problems, 56*(1), 49–69.

Salazar v. Edwards (1996). Settlement Stipulation. Circuit Court of Cook County, Illinois, County Department, Chancery Division. Case No. 92 CH 5703. Chicago, IL.

Salazar v. Edwards (1999). Memorandum of Opinion. Judge M. B. Getty, Circuit Court of Cook County, Illinois. County Department, Chancery Division, Case No. 92 CH 5703, Chicago, IL.

Salazar v. Edwards (2000). Settlement agreement and stipulation to dismiss. Circuit Court of Cook County, Illinois. County Department, Chancery Division. Case No. 92 CH 5703. Chicago, IL.

Salazar v. Edwards (2004). Motion of plaintiffs homeless children and parents for injunctive and declaratory relief to enforce settlement agreement. Circuit Court of Cook County, Illinois. County Department, Chancery Division. Case No. 92 CH 5703. Chicago, IL.

Schwandt, T. A. (1997). *Qualitative inquiry: A dictionary of terms.* Thousand Oaks, CA: Sage.

Sloss, C., & Bowhay, A. (2014). 22,144 homeless students enrolled in Chicago Public Schools this past year. *Chicago Coalition for the Homeless.* Retrieved from www.chicagohomeless.org/22144-cps-students/

Solórzano, D., & Yosso, T. (2002). Critical race methodology: Counter-storytelling as an analytical framework for education research. *Qualitative Inquiry, 8*(1), 23–44.

Soss, J., Fording, R. C., & Schram, S. F. (2011). *Disciplining the poor: Neoliberal paternalism and the persistent power of race.* Chicago, IL: University of Chicago Press.

Stewart B. McKinney Homeless Assistance Act of 1987, Pub. L. 100-77. 101 § 11431-35 Stat.525, 42 U.S.C. (1987).

Stovall, D. (2006). Forging community in race and class: Critical race theory and the quest for social justice in education. *Race, Ethnicity and Education, 9*(3), 243–259.

Tate, W. F., IV. (1997). Critical race theory and education: History, theory, and implications. *Review of Research in Education, 22*, 195–247.

United Nations. (1948). *The Universal Declaration of Human Rights.* Retrieved from www.un.org/en/documents/udhr/

U.S. Department of Education, Planning and Evaluation Service, Elementary and Secondary Education Division. (2002). *The Education for Homeless Children and Youth Program: Learning to Succeed: Vol. 2. Educating homeless children and youth: A resource guide to promising practices: Final report.* Washington, DC: Author.

U.S. Department of Housing and Urban Development, Office of Community Planning and Development. (2010). *The 2009 annual homeless assessment report to Congress* (5th Report). Washington, DC: Author.

United States Interagency Council on Homelessness (USICH). (2013, February). *Framework to end youth homelessness: A resource text for dialogue and action.* Washington, DC: Author.

Valenzuela, A. (1999). *Subtractive schooling: U.S. Mexican youth and the politics of caring.* Albany: State University of New York Press.

Vaught, S. (2011). *Racism, public schooling, and the entrenchment of White supremacy: A critical race ethnography.* Albany: State University of New York Press.

Vissing, Y., & Diament, J. (1997). Housing distress among high school students. *Social Work, 42*(1), 31–41.

Vostanis, P. (1999). Child mental health problems. In P. Vostanis & S. Cumella (Eds.), *Homeless children: Problems and needs* (pp. 43–54). London, England: Kingsley.

Vostanis, P., Grattan, E., & Cumella, S. (1998). Mental health problems of homeless children and families: Longitudinal study. *British Medical Journal, 316,* 899–902.

Wildman, S. M., & Davis, A. D. (2005). Making systems of privilege visible. In P. S. Rothenberg (Ed.), *White privilege: Essential readings on the other side of racism* (2nd ed., pp. 89–95). New York, NY: Worth.

Wilson, W. J. (1987). *The declining significance of race: Blacks and changing American institutions.* Chicago, IL: University of Chicago Press.

Winant, H. (2004). *The new politics of race: Globalism, difference and justice.* Minneapolis, MN: University of Minnesota Press.

Wong, J., Elliott, L. T., Reed, S., Ross, W., McGuirk, P., & Tallarita, L. (2009). McKinney–Vento Homeless Assistance Act Subtitle B—Education for Homeless Children and Youths Program: Turning good law into effective education, 2008 update. *Georgetown Journal on Poverty Law & Policy, 16,* 53–98.

Yosso, T. (2005). Whose culture has capital? A critical race theory discussion of community cultural wealth. *Race, Ethnicity and Education, 8*(1), 69–91.

Index

Unstable housing, 11
Unstably housed. See Homelessness
Urban centers statistics, 13
U.S. Department of Education, 7
U.S. Department of Housing and Urban
    Development, 8

Valenzuela, A., 107
Vaught, S., 17–18, 101
Violence threat, 23, 25, 27, 29, 37
Vissing, Y., 43
Vostanis, P., 9, 10

Waught, S. E., 8
Weissburg, R. P., 71

"White Privilege: Unpacking the
    Invisible Knapsack," 87
White supremacy, 99
Wildman, S. M., 16
Wilson, K., 9
Wilson, W. J., 12, 90
Winant, H., 16, 73
Wong, J., 65
Woods, A., 9

Yosso, T., 15, 17, 97
Yousafzai, Malala, 88
Youth participants in this research,
    108–109. *See also by name*
Youth policy input, 88–89, 107

About the Author

Ann Aviles de Bradley is an assistant professor in the Department of Educational Inquiry and Curriculum Studies at Northeastern Illinois University. Her research focuses on examining policies, services, and programs that impact the educational opportunities and mental health of homeless youth of color. Her research also addresses the topics of Latina/o education, education policy, educational equity, school–community partnerships, Critical Race Theory, youth development, and mental health. Dr. Aviles de Bradley's recent publications include "Homeless Educational Policy: Exploring a Racialized Discourse Through a Critical Race Theory Lens" in *Urban Education*. She currently teaches undergraduate and graduate courses in the Educational Foundations program at Northeastern Illinois University.